Test Your Brain Power

D1321939

Test Your Brain Power

Alan Wareham

WARD LOCK

To Alan and Neil

A WARD LOCK BOOK

First published in the UK in 1994
by Ward Lock
A Cassell Imprint
Villiers House
41/47 Strand
London WC2N 5JE

This book was previously published in two separate volumes. In the UK
the titles were *A Mensa Book of Brain Teasers* and *A Mensa Book of
Logic Puzzles*. In the US the titles were *A Challenging Book of Brain
Teasers* and *A Challenging Book of Logic Puzzles*.

Distributed in the United States
by Sterling Publishing Co., Inc.
387 Park Avenue South, New York, NY 10016-8810

Distributed in Australia
by Capricorn Link (Australia) Pty Ltd
2/13 Carrington Road, Castle Hill, NSW 2154

British Library Cataloguing-in-Publication Data
A catalogue record for this book is available from the British Library

ISBN 0-7063-7250-6

Typeset by Litho Link Ltd, Welshpool, Powys
Printed and bound in Great Britain by
Cox & Wyman Ltd, Reading, Berkshire

Acknowledgement

A special thanks to my wife Tracey for her help
in checking the questions, and for her
everlasting support and optimism.

CONTENTS

INTRODUCTION

What is brain power? How do you test it? Generally, brain power – or intelligence – is tested by means of short questions based on mathematics, logic and language, set against a time scale. Your answers are then compared to an average score, which will show how far above or below average you are. Many of the questions in this book are more complex and involved than those in the standard intelligence test and there is more 'to get your teeth into'. As a result, some may take a long time to answer, so there are no set time limits. However, the questions do have a star rating to enable you to monitor your performance:

* Easy
** Average
*** Challenging
**** Difficult
***** Very Difficult

Ratings aside, my main intention is that you enjoy answering the questions. Each puzzle has been cross-referenced with two numbers, a question number (Q) and an answer number (A). This means that you can check the answer to a question without the possibility of accidentally seeing the answer to the next question.

QUESTIONS

Q1 Paint-by-Numbers★ A30
Shown below is a 'Modern Art' paint-by-numbers grid. You only have four different colours and must not paint two adjoining sections, including the border, the same colour. Which two of the twelve numbered sections will be the same colour as the border?

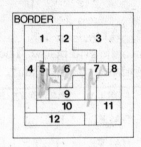

Q2 Who's Who?★ A41
Harry and Fred are called Smith and Jones, but I'm not sure if it's Harry Smith and Fred Jones or Harry Jones and Fred Smith. Given that two of the following statements are false, what is Harry's surname?

1. Harry's surname is Jones.
2. Harry's surname is Smith.
3. Fred's surname is Smith.

Q3 Card Sharp★ A61
Row 1 = Four cards with different letters on both sides.
Row 2 = The same four cards from Row 1, two of which have been turned over, all four of which are in different positions.
Row 3 = The same four cards from Row 2, two more of

which have been turned over, and all four of which are again in different positions to the positions they were in in Rows 1 and 2.

Which letter is on the other side of each of the four cards in Row 3?

ROW
1	A	B	C	D
2	H	G	A	C
3	E	F	G	H

Q4 Grid Fill★★ A10

Fit the 36 words into the grid below. The letter R has been entered into the grid for you as a start.

ADORN	AMPLE	AORTA	ARROW	BESET	BLAME
CLAMP	DALLY	DAZED	ELDER	EPOCH	EXACT
FILET	GALEA	HALVE	HAZEL	INDUE	IRATE
JAUNT	JOINT	MADAM	OCTAL	OPERA	REDID
REFER	RIDGE	RODEO	ROYAL	SEPIA	SPRAT
SURGE	TERSE	THEIR	THEME	TREAT	UNDER

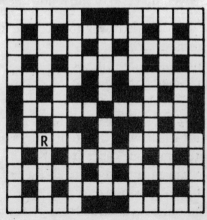

Q5 Every Which Way★ A69

There are two different ways of completing a 4 × 4 grid so that all four columns, rows and both diagonals contain the numbers 1, 2, 3 and 4, and the top row contains the numbers in ascending order. What are they?

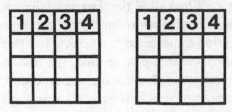

Q6 Flipover★★★ A104

Diagram One is that of the numbers 1, 2, 3 and 4; each of which is surrounded by eight circles, all of which contain a different letter. The eight circles around each of the four numbers can be 'flipped over' the number itself either vertically or horizontally. For example, in diagram One, if the letters around the number 1 were flipped vertically, A and F would swap places, B and G would swap places, C and H would swap places and D and E would remain in the same position.

Diagram Two is that of Diagram One after each of the four numbers have been flipped over either vertically or horizontally. In which direction have the letters around each number been flipped over to arrive at the positions shown in diagram Two?

Diagram One

(A) (D) (F) (I) (K) (N) (P) (S) (U)
(B) (1) (G) (2) (L) (3) (Q) (4) (V)
(C) (E) (H) (J) (M) (O) (R) (T) (W)

Diagram Two

(F) (D) (C) (J) (K) (O) (U) (S) (R)
(G) (1) (B) (2) (L) (3) (V) (4) (Q)
(H) (E) (A) (I) (M) (N) (W) (T) (P)

Q7 Laser Maze*** A80

The diagram below represents an aerial view of a room which has been divided into 100 squares, as shown by the dotted lines. In each of the squares there should be a dot marked on the floor in the centre of the square, or a double-sided mirror. When all of the dots and mirrors are in their correct places, a laser beam can enter the room at square A1 in the direction indicated by an arrow, and leave the room from square J10. At the same time, the laser beam shines over each and every dot marked on the floor. When the beam reaches a mirror it 'bounces off' at an angle of 90°, but it never crosses itself. If the beam hits the outside wall it is absorbed by the wall and can go no further.

Fourteen of the dots/mirrors are not in place: five dots (X), six mirrors from lower left to upper right (Y), and three mirrors from upper left to lower right (Z). See if you can determine which of the squares containing '?' should be replaced by:

1. X squares; 2. Y squares; 3. Z squares.

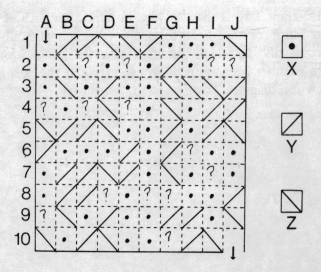

Q8 Stationary Stationery** A90

The other day, the stationery clerk asked George, Fred and Arthur if they would carry some parcels of stationery to the typists' office. There were six parcels in all: one large parcel, which weighed the same as the two medium-sized parcels, which in turn weighed the same as the three small parcels. The stationery clerk then said that one person could carry the large parcel, one person could carry the two medium-sized parcels and one person could carry the three small parcels; that way all three would be carrying the same weight of stationery. George, Fred and Arthur weren't very happy about having to carry the stationery anyway and said that they would only carry the stationery to the typists on the following conditions.

George would only carry the two medium-sized parcels if Fred carried the three small parcels. Fred would only carry the three small parcels if George carried the large parcel. George would only carry the large parcel if Arthur carried the two medium-sized parcels. Arther would only carry the two medium-sized parcels if Fred carried the large parcel. George would only carry the three small parcels if Arthur carried the large parcel. All this time the stationery remained stationary. Eventually the stationery clerk came up with a solution to keep all three happy. Who carried what to the typists?

Q9 Letter Boxes★ A115

When the diagram below is complete, each column and row should contain the letters A, B, C, D, E, F, G, H, I and J. See if you can complete the diagram by fitting the nine blocks of nine letters into the nine highlighted squares, then filling in the spaces along the top row and in the first column.

	F		J		B	
E						
A						
H						

D	I	B
J	H	F
A	F	J

J	E	H
C	D	G
E	G	I

C	A	D
F	J	H
I	D	E

C	G	A
B	A	I
D	H	C

B	H	F
D	I	E
G	F	A

B	C	G
H	E	C
E	G	I

H	A	D
A	B	J
F	C	B

J	E	G
G	C	B
H	B	J

F	I	E
I	D	F
A	J	D

Q10 Logic Box★ A20

Using the following clues, place the letters A to I inclusive into the grid. G is above I and to the right of B. C is to the right of H and above I which is to the left of D. B is to the left of E. H is above F and B. A is above E. ('Above' refers to two letters in the same column. 'Left of/right of' refers to two letters in the same row.)

12

Q11 What Next?* A124

Find the next most appropriate square:

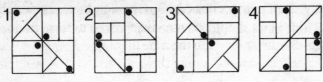

Choose from:

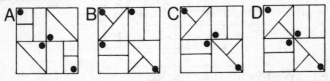

Q12 Blocked*** A134

Each of the 25 blocks of four letters shown below can be rotated about its centre, either 90° clockwise or 90° anti-clockwise. When all of the 25 blocks are in their correct positions, all ten rows and columns contain the letters A to J only once.

Twelve of the blocks shown below are not in their correct positions. Six blocks have been rotated clockwise and six blocks have been rotated anticlockwise. Given that at least two blocks, and no more than three blocks, have been rotated in each of the five rows and columns of blocks, which 12 of the 25 have been rotated and in which direction?

	A	B	C	D	E
1	C A / D E	D F / F J	G H / B C	I B / H I	G J / A E
2	I C / E B	H I / A G	J B / H D	G D / F A	F C / E J
3	J D / F H	B G / D A	A J / F C	E G / C E	H I / I B
4	A G / J F	C J / I B	E F / I E	D B / H C	D A / G H
5	I B / H G	E H / C E	A G / D I	F J / J A	C D / B F

13

Q13 Square Cut★ A50

Divide the diagram into four parts of equal size and shape, each part of which must contain the numbers 1, 2, 3 and 4. The four parts should then be rearranged to form a square.

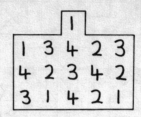

Q14 Wordsquare★ A139

Fit the 12 blocks into the grid to form a wordsquare which reads the same down and across.

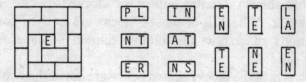

Q15 Odd One Out★ A1

Which of the six cubes shown cannot be constructed from the flattened cube below?

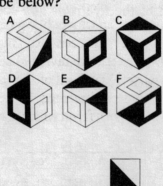

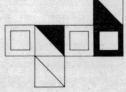

Q16 Connection★ A146

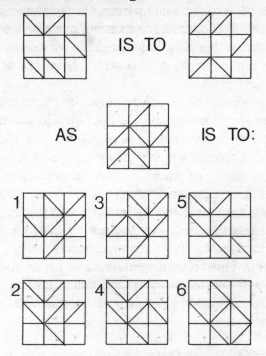

1 3 5

2 4 6

Q17 The History of Invention★★ A125

I had a list of various inventions which were in date order, but the piece of paper on which they were listed was torn in half, one half of which has been lost. Given the list of years in which the inventions were invented and the information below, see if you can match all of the inventions with the year in which they were invented.

This is the half I have left, on which is written the years of invention:

1320, 1607, 1710, 1721, 1763, 1764, 1783, 1815, 1841, 1856, 1868, 1876, 1877, 1898, 1899, 1935, 1939, 1941.

Gunpowder, the telescope, pianoforte and the mercury thermometer were all invented before the spinning jenny, the steam engine and the hot air balloon. Steel, the wireless and the sewing machine were all invented before radar and the tank. The miner's safety lamp, the telephone, gunpowder, steel, dynamite and the sewing machine were all invented before the phonograph and the wireless, the two of which, and the tank, were invented before radar, the jet engine and polyester.

Gunpowder, the spinning jenny, the steam engine, the mercury thermometer and the hot air balloon were all invented before the miner's safety lamp and the sewing machine. Polyester was invented after dynamite, radar and the jet engine. The pianoforte was invented after the telescope and gunpowder. Dynamite was invented after steel, the sewing machine and the miner's safety lamp.

Steel was invented after the sewing machine which in turn was invented after the miner's safety lamp. The wireless was invented after the phonograph, the jet engine after radar, and the telephone after dynamite. The spinning jenny was invented before the steam engine and the hot air balloon.

Q18   Odd Block Out*   A36
Which is the odd block out?

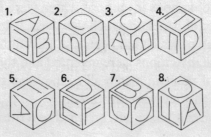

Q19   Done What?*   A105
Dave said Bill did it, Bill said Arthur did it, Arthur said Eddie did it, Eddie said Charlie did it and Charlie said that he didn't do it. If Charlie didn't do it, one of the five of them did do it and only one of them is telling the truth; who did do it?

Q20 Number Fill★ A70

Given that the same number does not appear in two adjacent squares, either vertically, horizontally or diagonally, fit the numbers 1 to 9 inclusive four times each into the 6 × 6 grid. Only one number should be entered into each of the 36 squares. The numbers appear next to the row and beneath the column into which they should be placed.

							1 3 4 5 7 9
							1 2 3 8 8 9
							2 3 4 4 6 6
							1 5 5 7 7 8
							1 2 2 6 9 9
							3 4 5 6 7 8

```
2 1 2 2 1 1
5 1 3 5 2 3
5 3 7 6 4 3
5 4 7 6 4 6
9 8 7 9 4 6
9 8 8 9 8 7
```

Q21 Where Do They Live?★★ A144

There are five houses in a street, numbered 1, 2, 3, 4 and 5, each with one resident. Given the seven lists of five surnames and the house in which each of them resides, see if you can determine the surname of the five residents and the number of the house in which each resides. There is a catch, as you may have noticed already: not all seven lists are the same, therefore they cannot all be correct. In fact none of the lists are completely correct. The number at the bottom of each list is the number of resident(s) whose surnames have been listed next to the correct house number.

House no.	A	B	C	D	E	F	G
1	Brown	Smith	Allen	Smith	Brown	Duffy	Duffy
2	Coates	Johnson	Dodds	Dodds	Coates	Dodds	Johnson
3	Anderson	Russell	Finlay	Anderson	Finlay	Williams	Williams
4	Carter	Morris	Bainbridge	Morris	Morris	Arthur	Parker
5	McDonald	Charlton	Humphries	Grant	Grant	Charlton	Scott
	(Two)	(Two)	(One)	(One)	(One)	(One)	(One)

17

Q22   Every Which Way★   A51

There are two different ways of completing a 5 × 5 grid so that all five columns, rows and both diagonals contain the numbers 1, 2, 3, 4 and 5; the top row contains the numbers in ascending order; and no diagonal line of two or more squares contains the same number more than once. What are they? (The number 1 has been placed in the first grid as a start.)

Q23   Logic Box★   A62

Using the following clues, place the letters A to I inclusive into the grid. C is below G and above E. D is above A and to the right of F which is above I and to the left of G. A is above H and to the right of I. H is to the right of B and to the left of E. ('Above/below' refers to two letters in the same column. 'Left of/right of' refers to two letters in the same row.)

Q24 Grid Fill★★ A91

Fit the 36 words into the grid below. The letters A and I have been entered into the grid for you as a start.

ALLIN ASSAI ATRIP AUDIO BARGE CAIRD

CHANT CHILD DECAL DIVOT DRAIL ENTRY

ESSAY EXERT FEAST INLET IONIC LOCAL

MULTI NEEDY NIECE OCTAL ODEON OMBRE

OMEGA OPTIC OUNCE PILAU RADIO REFER

RELIC TAINT TEMPO TOTAL TWIRL VRAIC

Q25 The Mad Hatter** A11

Last week the Mad Hatter wore a different style of hat on each day, and each hat was a different colour. Given the following 14 statements, on which day did the Mad Hatter wear the top hat and what colour was the fez?

1. The blue hat was worn on Monday.
2. The cap is yellow.
3. The fez was not worn on Monday or Tuesday.
4. The stetson was worn before the bowler hat and the top hat.
5. The fez is not black.
6. The orange hat was worn before the black hat and after the trilby.
7. The sombrero is not red or blue.
8. The trilby was worn the day after the bowler hat.
9. The black hat was worn on Saturday or Sunday.
10. The trilby is green and the first day of the week is Monday.
11. The top hat is not black or red.
12. The white hat was worn before the fez and after the yellow hat.
13. The bowler hat was not worn on Friday or Saturday.
14. The cap was worn after the trilby and before the fez.

Q26 Odd Ones Out* A79

Which three cubes cannot be made from the flattened cube shown below?

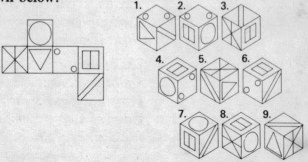

20

Q27   Before or Not Before*** A42

My wife Tracey is very keen on English Literature, and has read most of the works of Shakespeare, the last one being *Richard III*. I asked Tracey for a list of the works of Shakespeare that she had read so that I could use the list in a puzzle, but she gave me the list in the following form. Each play she had read was listed on the left-hand side. On the right-hand side was one or more of the plays that she had read after the play shown on the left-hand side. It is possible to construct a list of the plays in the order that my wife read them; what is the correct order?

Play	*Plays read after play shown to the left*
The Taming of the Shrew	*A Midsummer Night's Dream, The Comedy of Errors, The Merchant of Venice, Twelfth Night, Antony and Cleopatra.*
Romeo and Juliet	*As You Like It, Julius Caesar, Troilus and Cressida, The Tempest, Much Ado About Nothing, The Winter's Tale.*
Much Ado About Nothing	*Twelfth Night, The Taming of the Shrew, The Tempest, The Comedy of Errors, King John.*
The Comedy of Errors	*Coriolanus, King John, Twelfth Night, Macbeth, Cymbeline, A Midsummer Night's Dream.*
Julius Caesar	*The Taming of the Shrew, A Midsummer Night's Dream, Merry Wives of Windsor, Timon of Athens, Hamlet, The Comedy of Errors,*

continued overleaf

	The Merchant of Venice, Love's Labour's Lost.
Measure for Measure	*Love's Labour's Lost, Hamlet, All's Well That Ends Well, Timon of Athens, The Taming of the Shrew, Twelfth Night.*
The Merchant of Venice	*Hamlet, The Tempest.*
Love's Labour's Lost	*Troilus and Cressida.*
Hamlet	*Antony and Cleopatra.*
Cymbeline	*A Midsummer Night's Dream.*
The Winter's Tale	*All's Well That Ends Well, Antony and Cleopatra, King John, Measure for Measure, Troilus and Cressida, Much Ado About Nothing.*
Two Gentlemen of Verona	*As You Like It, Romeo and Juliet, The Winter's Tale.*
Merry Wives of Windsor	*The Winter's Tale, Much Ado About Nothing, Timon of Athens.*
The Tempest	*The Comedy of Errors, Twelfth Night.*
Timon of Athens	*Love's Labour's Lost.*
Titus Andronicus	*Two Gentlemen of Verona, Julius Caesar, Twelfth Night, The Winter's Tale, Romeo and Juliet.*
Troilus and Cressida	*Antony and Cleopatra, Much Ado About Nothing.*

continued opposite

Twelfth Night	*A Midsummer Night's Dream, Coriolanus, Cymbeline, Macbeth.*
All's Well That Ends Well	*Love's Labour's Lost, Timon of Athens.*
Antony and Cleopatra	*The Tempest.*
As You Like It	*Julius Caesar, The Winter's Tale, Much Ado About Nothing.*
Coriolanus	*Macbeth.*
King John	*Twelfth Night.*
Macbeth	*Cymbeline, A Midsummer Night's Dream.*

Q28   Auntie Christmas★★   A25

1. Auntie Carol will not get the flowers unless Auntie Sheila gets the chocolates.
2. Auntie Sheila will not get the chocolates unless Auntie Joan gets the slippers.
3. Auntie Mary will not get the flowers unless Auntie Joan gets the chocolates.
4. Auntie Joan will not get the slippers unless Auntie Carol gets the chocolates.
5. Auntie Joan will not get the voucher unless Auntie Sheila gets the slippers.
6. Auntie Sheila will not get the slippers unless Auntie Mary gets the flowers.
7. Auntie Mary will not get the voucher unless Auntie Carol gets the slippers.
8. Auntie Carol will not get the voucher unless Auntie Sheila gets the flowers.
9. Auntie Sheila will not get the flowers unless Auntie Joan gets the slippers.

continued overleaf

23

10.   Auntie Sheila will not get the voucher unless Auntie Carol gets the slippers.

11.   Auntie Carol will not get the slippers unless Auntie Joan gets the flowers.

Which Auntie will get the slippers for Christmas?

Q29   Blocked***   A2

Each of the 25 blocks of four letters shown below can be rotated about its centre, either 90° clockwise or 90° anti-clockwise. When all of the 25 blocks are in their correct positions, all ten rows and columns contain the letters A to J only once.

Fifteen of the blocks shown below are not in their correct positions. Seven blocks have been rotated clockwise and eight blocks have been rotated anticlockwise. Given that three blocks have been rotated in each of the five rows and columns of blocks, which 15 of the 25 have been rotated and in which direction?

	A	B	C	D	E
1	I F / G E	J H / A B	E G / F H	C A / I C	D B / J D
2	B D / D H	B H / J E	G J / A C	F I / G F	A I / E C
3	G J / J A	F I / C E	D H / C B	B D / A H	I E / F G
4	C A / H C	I G / F D	E B / I J	B D / G E	J H / A F
5	F I / E B	C A / D G	A F / I D	E J / J H	H B / G C

Q30   Square Cut*   A31

Divide the square into four parts of equal size and shape, each of which must include the nine letters, S, E, C, T, I, O, N, A and L.

```
C L I S T C
A O E N I A
L N S A C S
T I C L N O
E O A O S E
N T I E L T
```

Q31 Done What?* A126

Arthur said Dave did it, Dave said Bill did it, Bill said Charlie did it, Charlie said that he didn't do it and Eddie confessed that he did it. If Arthur didn't do it, one of the five of them did do it and only one of them is telling the truth; who did do it?

Q32 Letter Boxes* A143

When the diagram below is complete, each column and row should contain the letters A, B, C, D, E, F, G, H, I and J. See if you can complete the diagram by fitting the nine blocks of nine letters into the nine highlighted squares and filling in the remaining spaces.

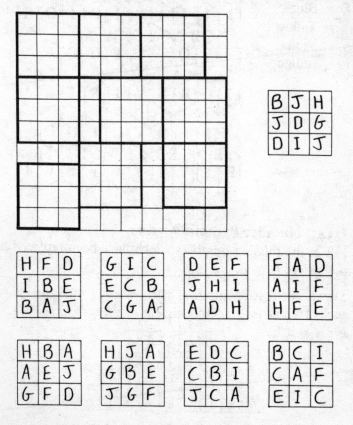

Q33 Colour Cube★ A92

A large cube can be made with the 27 smaller cubes shown below, so that each face of the large cube is entirely red, orange, green, yellow, blue or violet.

The faces of the smaller cubes that you cannot see are indigo. Which cubes could be on the top layer, which in the centre layer and which on the bottom layer? Put the numbers of the cubes (left to right, top to bottom) in three 9-box grids. To start you off, nos 1 and 23 are in the top layer.

R = Red
O = Orange
G = Green
B = Blue
Y = Yellow
V = Violet
I = Indigo

Q34 Number Pyramid★ A71

Fill in the missing numbers which have been replaced by the letters A to F.

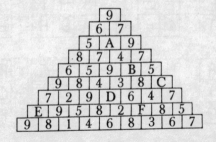

Q35 Flipover*** A106

Diagram One is that of the numbers 1, 2, 3 and 4, each of which is surrounded by eight circles, all of which contain a different letter. The eight circles around each of the four numbers can be 'flipped over' the number itself either vertically or horizontally. For example, in Diagram One, if the letters around the number 1 were flipped vertically, A and F would swap places, B and G would swap places, C and H would swap places and D and E would remain in the same position.

Diagram Two is that of Diagram One after each of the four numbers have been flipped over a total of six times. Each number has been flipped over at least once but no more than twice. In what order, and in which direction, have the letters around each number been flipped over to arrive at the positions shown in Diagram Two?

Diagram One

(A)(D)(F)(I)(K)(N)(P)(S)(U)
(B)(1)(G)(2)(L)(3)(Q)(4)(V)
(C)(E)(H)(J)(M)(O)(R)(T)(W)

Diagram Two

(C)(E)(F)(I)(M)(N)(W)(S)(R)
(B)(1)(G)(2)(L)(3)(V)(4)(Q)
(A)(D)(H)(J)(K)(O)(U)(T)(P)

Q36 Double Wordsquare* A12

Fit the 20 blocks into the two grids to form two different wordsquares which read the same down and across.

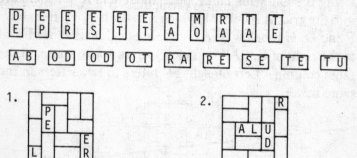

Q37 Connection*** A116

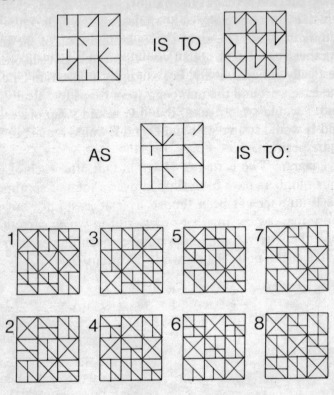

Q38 Logic Box* A21

Using the following clues, place the letters A to I inclusive into the grid. A is below E which is to the left of I. B is above F and D. H is below E and to the left of C. D is above F and to the right of G. ('Above/below' refers to two letters in the same column. 'Left of/right of' refers to two letters in the same row.)

Given below is a list of monarchs whose names all begin with the letter E. The list gives the names of some or all of the other monarchs who were monarchs after the monarch whose name is given first in Column One. All you have to do is construct a list of the monarchs in the order in which they became monarchs. As there were quite a few Edwards, if you were given the information as Edward I, Edward II, Edward III etc., it would be too easy; so the Edwards have had their numbers replaced by the number of years they were king. The Elizabeths have been left unchanged.

Column One *Name of monarch*	*Column Two* *Monarchs who were monarchs after the monarch in column One*
Edward the Confessor	Edward (1 year), Edward (35 years), Elizabeth I, Edward (10 years).
Ethelbald	Ethelbert, Ethelred, Ethelred the Unready, Edward (22 years), Edmund Ironside, Edmund.
Edmund Ironside	Elizabeth I, Edward the Confessor, Edward (22 years), Edward (1 year), Edward (6 years).
Edward the Elder	Edmund, Edmund Ironside, Edgar.
Edward (22 years)	Edward (1 year), Elizabeth I.
Edgar	Edward the Martyr.
Egbert	Ethelwulf, Ethelred, Elizabeth I, Edmund, Ethelbald.
Ethelred the Unready	Edward (10 years), Edmund Ironside.
Elizabeth I	Edward (9 years), Elizabeth II, Edward who abdicated.

continued overleaf

Edmund	Edwig, Edward (10 years), Edward (6 years), Edred, Ethelred the Unready, Edmund Ironside.
Ethelwulf	Ethelbert, Ethelbald, Edmund.
Edwig	Edward the Martyr, Edgar.
Edward (10 years)	Edward (22 years).
Ethelbert	Ethelred, Edmund, Edmund Ironside.
Edward (1 year)	Edward (9 years), Edward (6 years), Elizabeth I, Edward who abdicated, Elizabeth II.
Edward (9 years)	Edward who abdicated.
Ethelred	Edward the Confessor, Edward the Elder, Edgar, Edward (1 year), Edward (35 years), Edward the Martyr, Edward (20 years).
Edward (6 years)	Elizabeth I.
Edward who abdicated	Elizabeth II.
Edred	Edward the Martyr, Edward (20 years), Edwig, Edgar, Edward the Confessor, Elizabeth I.
Edward (35 years)	Edward (20 years), Edward (22 years).
Edward the Martyr	Ethelred the Unready.
Edward (20 years)	Edward (10 years).

Q40 Odd One Out★★★ A43

The diagrams below are that of a flattened cube and three views of the cube before it was flattened. Which of the three views is incorrect? (The cube can be restored to its original form by folding along the dotted lines. None of the three views show the edges of the diagram of the flattened cube.)

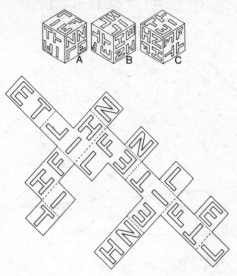

Q41 Laser Maze★★★ A52

The diagram on page 32 represents an aerial view of a room which has been divided into 100 squares, as shown by the dotted lines. In each of the squares there should be a dot marked on the floor in the centre of the square, or a double-sided mirror. When all of the dots and mirrors are in their correct places, a laser beam can enter the room at square A1 in the direction indicated by an arrow, and leave the room from square J10. At the same time, the laser beam shines over each and every dot marked on the floor. When the beam reaches a mirror it 'bounces off' at an angle of 90°, but it never crosses itself. If the beam hits the outside wall it is absorbed by the wall and can go no further. In the room below only one side of a mirror is ever used.

Fourteen of the dots/mirrors are not in place: four dots (X), seven mirrors from lower left to upper right (Y), and three mirrors from upper left to lower right (Z). See if you can determine which of the squares containing '?' should be replaced by: 1. X squares; 2. Y squares; 3. Z squares.

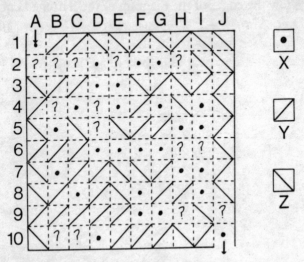

Q42   All The Twos*   A127

Alex, Brad, Colin, Doug, Eric and Frank had a race to school from the bus-stop and then another race from school to the bus-stop. In the first race, Brad wasn't last and Eric finished before Colin. Frank wasn't first but finished before Doug. Brad finished before Frank but after Alex and Colin. Alex finished four places ahead of Doug. In the second race Alex finished two places ahead of Doug and after Eric who in turn was two places behind Colin. Alex wasn't first and nor was Brad who finished before Eric. Frank finished one place ahead of Doug.

From the information given:

1. Which two boys finished in a better position in the first race than in the second race?

2. Which two boys finished in the same position in the second race as they did in the first race?

32

Q43 People's Pets* A93

Consider the following.

1. Five men each have different first names and different surnames, have five different pets and live at five different addresses. All five pets have a different name.

2. Tom's surname is Williams and the fish is not called Spike, Benson or Rodney.

3. Harry has a pet cat and the budgie is called Percy.

4. George's surname is not Hudson or Smith.

5. Mr Thompson owns the dog and the owner of the rabbit lives in Pine Avenue.

6. The cat is not called Benson and one of the five men has a pet called Fred.

7. Mr Anderson does not live in Cedar Road.

8. Mr Hudson lives in Willow Street.

9. Mr Anderson owns a pet called Percy and John lives in Cedar Road.

10. Bill's pet is called Rodney and is not the dog; the owner of the fish lives in Maple Grove.

Who lives in Chestnut Crescent and what is the name of their pet?

Q44 The Animals Went In Which Way?*** A63

The animals may have gone into Noah's Ark two by two, but in which order did they go in? Given the following sentence (yes, sentence! – I make no apologies for the punctuation), what was the order in which the animals entered the Ark?

The monkeys went in before the sheep, swans, chickens, peacocks, geese, penguins and spiders, but went in after the horses, badgers, squirrels and tigers, the latter of which went in before the horses, the penguins, the rabbits, the pigs, the donkeys, the snakes and the mice, but the mice went before the leopards, the leopards before the squirrels, the squirrels before the chickens, the chickens before the penguins, spiders, sheep, geese and the peacocks, the peacocks before the geese and the penguins, the penguins before the spiders and after the geese and the horses, the horses before the donkeys, the chickens and the leopards, the leopards after the foxes and the ducks, the ducks before the goats, swans, doves, foxes and badgers, the badgers before the chickens, horses, squirrels and swans and after the lions, foxes, rabbits and beavers, the beavers before the lions, tigers, foxes, squirrels and ducks, the ducks after the lions, elephants, rabbits and otters, the otters before the elephants, tigers, chickens and beavers, the beavers after the elephants, the elephants before the lions, the lions before the tigers, the sheep before the peacocks, the swans before the chickens, the pigs before the snakes, the snakes before the foxes, the pigs after the rabbits, goats, tigers and doves, the doves before the chickens, horses, goats, donkeys and snakes, the snakes after the goats, and the donkeys before the mice and the squirrels.

Q45 Mix Up Square* A3

Complete the square so that all of the columns and rows contain the letters:

S Q U A R E

Each of the six letters must only appear once in each column or row.

S	Q	U	A	R	E
E					
Q	E			A	
A			S		
	U				Q
		R		E	S

Q46 Odd Block Out* A137
Which is the odd block out?

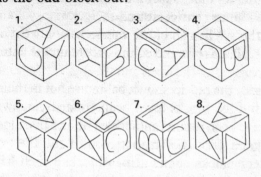

Q47 Grid Fill*** A37
Fit the 36 words into the grid below.

ALLOT   AMENT   AMORT   ARISE   ATLAS   CAROL

DOLCE   ELDER   EMEND   EVENS   EVENT   EXILE

HAREM   IDLER   IMAGE   LATER   LINER   NEWEL

NOISE   OKAPI   OPINE   REVUE   RINSE   ROOST

SOWER   SPENT   STALE   TATER   THEIR   THEME

TREAT   VENUE   VILLA   VISIT   YEAST   YODEL

Q48 Blocked*** A145

Each of the 25 blocks of four letters shown below can be rotated about its centre, either 90° clockwise, 90° anticlockwise or 180°. When all of the 25 blocks are in their correct positions, all ten rows and columns contain the letters A to J only once.

Fifteen of the blocks shown below are not in their correct positions. Five blocks have been rotated clockwise, five blocks have been rotated anticlockwise and five blocks have been rotated 180°. Given that each of the five rows and columns of blocks contain three blocks which have been rotated, no two of which have been rotated the same way, which 15 of the 25 have been rotated and in which direction?

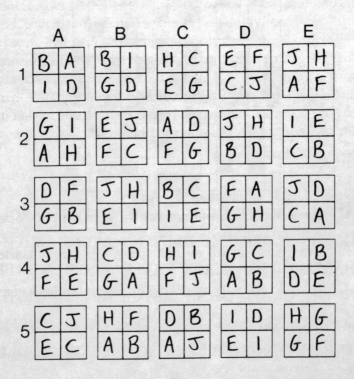

Q49 Logicalympics – 100 Metres** A107

The logicalympics take place every year in a very quiet setting so that the competitors can concentrate on their events – not so much the events themselves, but the results. At the logicalympics every event ends in a tie so that no one goes home disappointed. There were five entries in the 100m, so they held five races in order that each competitor could win, and so that each competitor could also take his/her turn in 2nd, 3rd, 4th and 5th place. The final results showed that each competitor had duly taken their turn in finishing in each of the five positions. Given the following information, what were the results of each of the five races?

The five competitors were A, B, C, D and E. C didn't win the fourth race. In the first race A finished before C who in turn finished after B. A finished in a better position in the fourth race than in the second race. E didn't win the second race. E finished two places behind C in the first race. D lost the fourth race. A finished ahead of B in the fourth race, but B finished before A and C in the third race. A had already finished before C in the second race who in turn finished after B again. B was not first in the first race and D was not last. D finished in a better position in the second race than in the first race and finished before B. A wasn't second in the second race and also finished before B.

Q50 Uncle Christmas** A117

1. Uncle Raymond will not get the scarf unless Uncle John gets the hat.
2. Uncle George will not get the gloves unless Uncle Victor gets the scarf.
3. Uncle Victor will not get the tie unless Uncle George gets the scarf.
4. Uncle John will not get the gloves unless Uncle Raymond gets the hat.

continued overleaf

5. Uncle John will not get the hat unless Uncle Victor gets the gloves.

6. Uncle George will not get the hat unless Uncle Raymond gets the tie.

7. Uncle George will not get the tie unless Uncle Raymond gets the hat.

8. Uncle Raymond will not get the hat unless Uncle George gets the scarf.

9. Uncle Victor will not get the gloves unless Uncle Raymond gets the hat.

10. Uncle John will not get the tie unless Uncle Raymond gets the gloves.

11. Uncle George will not get the scarf unless Uncle Raymond gets the gloves.

Which Uncle will get the scarf for Christmas?

Q51 Number Fill* A72

Given that the same number does not appear in two adjacent squares, either vertically, horizontally or diagonally, fit the numbers 1 to 9 inclusive four times each into the 6 × 6 grid. Only one number should be entered into each of the 36 squares. Some of the numbers appear next to the row and/or beneath the column into which they should be placed.

						5 6 9
						2 2 3 7 8
						5 5 6
						2 2 3 9 7
						1 4 5 8 8
						3 3 6 7 9 9

4	1	1	2	1	1
4	2	6	2	6	3
7	2	6	3	7	3
8	5	9	5	8	4
8	7	9	5	8	4
9	7	9	5		

Q52 Coin Puzzle★ A53

Move one coin so that there are two straight lines of six coins which cross each other at the centre point of each line.

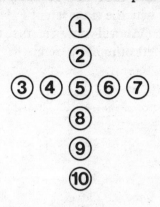

Q53 Clockwork★★★ A140

Diagram One is that of the numbers 1, 2, 3 and 4, each of which is surrounded by eight circles, all of which contain a different letter. The eight circles around each of the four numbers can be rotated either 90° clockwise, 90° anticlockwise or 180°. For example, if 1 were to be rotated 90° clockwise, the letter A would replace the letter F, D would replace G, F would replace H, G would replace E, H would replace C, etc.

Diagram Two is that of Diagram One after seven rotations of the letters around the four numbers – two clockwise, two anticlockwise and three through 180°. The letters around each number have been rotated at least once but no more than twice. In what order, and in which direction, have the letters around each number been rotated in Diagram One to arrive at the position shown in Diagram Two?

Diagram One

Ⓐ Ⓓ Ⓕ Ⓘ Ⓚ Ⓝ Ⓟ Ⓢ Ⓤ
Ⓑ ① Ⓖ ② Ⓛ ③ Ⓠ ④ Ⓥ
Ⓒ Ⓔ Ⓗ Ⓙ Ⓜ Ⓞ Ⓡ Ⓣ Ⓦ

Diagram Two

Ⓕ Ⓔ Ⓐ Ⓑ Ⓦ Ⓥ Ⓡ Ⓠ Ⓟ
① ① Ⓖ ② Ⓝ ③ Ⓣ ④ Ⓢ
Ⓚ Ⓓ Ⓤ Ⓞ Ⓜ Ⓙ Ⓗ Ⓛ Ⓒ

Q54 Logic Box★ A94

Using the following clues, place the letters A to I inclusive into the grid. E is to the right of C. A is to the right of G which is above B which is to the left of F. I is above D which is to the left of G. ('Above/below' refers to two letters in the same column. 'Left of/right of' refers to two letters in the same row.)

Q55 What Next?★ A13

Find the next most appropriate square:

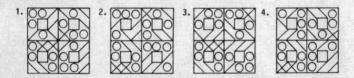

Choose from:

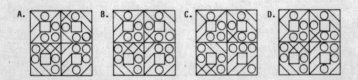

Q56 Grouping★ A44

To which group does the letter J belong?

1. F G
2. B C D E
3. A
4. H I

40

Neil is younger than Matthew. Barry is older than Robert and Dave. Dave is older than Joe who is younger than John and Philip. Arthur is older than Paul who is older than Matthew. Robert is older than Dave. Martin is older than Simon. George is also older than Simon but younger than Martin. Bill is older than Jimmy and Tom but younger than Harry. Harry is also older than Tom. Tom is older than Arthur, Dave and Eddie but younger than Jimmy. Keith is older than Barry. Neil is younger than Kevin and older than Frank. Paul is also older than Frank. Simon is older than Ian. Ian is older than Neil and Colin. Colin is older than John but younger than Eddie. Kevin is older than Martin and Michael.

John is younger than Michael. Keith and Dave are younger than John. Philip is older than Keith. Jimmy and Bill are younger than Leonard. Harry is older than Leonard. Michael and John are younger than Philip. Philip is older than Barry. Arthur is older than Neil. Frank and Colin are younger than Bill. John is older than Robert. Robert is younger than Philip who is older than Dave. Arthur is also older than Dave. Kevin and Colin are younger than Jimmy. Leonard is older than Kevin who is younger than Bill. Ian is also younger than Bill. Tom is older than Paul, Simon and Matthew. Fred is also older than Simon and Matthew.

George is younger than Tom and Fred. Kevin is older than Fred and Colin. Colin is older than Arthur and Frank. Arthur is older than Philip. Philip is younger than Colin. Arthur, Frank and Fred are older than John. Eddie is older than Kevin and George. Colin is older than Michael. Philip and John are younger than Frank. Harry is older than Kevin. Barry is younger than John. Ian is younger than Kevin. Tom is older than Philip. Martin and Arthur are younger than Fred.

Using the information given above, list all of the people mentioned in order of age, oldest first.

Q58 Letter Boxes* A26

When the diagram below is complete, each column and row should contain the letters A, B, C, D, E, F, G, H, I and J. See if you can complete the diagram by fitting the nine blocks of nine letters into the nine highlighted squares and filling in the remaining spaces.

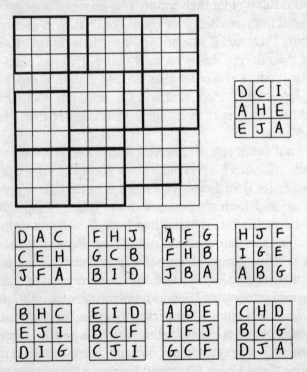

Q59 Done What?* A128

George said Arthur did it, Arthur said Bill did it, Bill said Charlie did it, Charlie said Fred did it, Eddie said Fred did it so Fred confessed and said that he did do it. Harry said Eddie did it, Dave then confessed and said that he did it so John also confessed and said that he did it. Finally, Ian said that he didn't do it. If George didn't do it, one of the ten of them did do it and only one of them is telling the truth; who did do it?

Q60 Connection*** A95

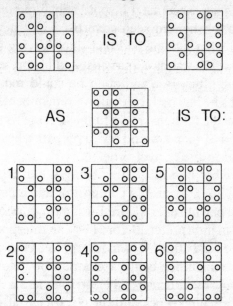

Q61 Safecracker* A135

The combination of a safe consists of the numbers 1, 2, 3 and 4. There are only the four numbers in the combination but the safe is computerised and changes the combination each time it is closed. Each number appears only once in each combination. The person opening the safe is only allowed four attempts, after which the safe cannot be opened for at least 48 hours. When you tap in the combination on the push-button panel, there is a display next to the panel which indicates the number of numbers you have 'tapped in' in the correct position. The last time that I opened the safe I tapped in the following combinations; on my first attempt I tapped in 3 1 2 4, none of which were in the correct place. I then tapped in 2 3 4 1; again none of the numbers were in the correct place. On my third attempt I only tapped in the number 1 in first place; the safe indicated that it was not in the correct place, after which I then knew the combination. What was the correct combination?

My friend Jack asked me if I would help him prepare a new C.V. for a job he had seen advertised in a newspaper. I asked him what jobs he had had since leaving school. He said his first job was as a journalist and his present job was as a scene-shifter, but, although he could remember the various jobs he had had, he couldn't remember the order in which he had had them. I told him to tell me what he could remember and then I would try to prepare a list of the jobs he had had in the correct order.

This is what he said: 'After being a journalist I was a signwriter, an illustrator, a compositor and a pawnbroker, but I was a pawnbroker before I was a ringmaster, a piano-tuner and an interpreter. Before I was an interpreter I was a chargehand, and after I was an interpreter I was a compositor. I can remember being a compositor before I was a gamekeeper, a taxi-driver, an electrician and a roadsweeper. I was a gamekeeper and an electrician after I was a roadsweeper which in turn was after I was a taxi-driver and a woodcarver. I liked my job as a woodcarver which I got after being a blacksmith, a chargehand, a lumberjack and an illustrator. I was an illustrator after I had a job as a cartoonist and an undertaker, and I was an undertaker before I was a pawnbroker and a chargehand but after I was a signwriter and a cartoonist.

'I can also remember being a fishmonger, a lumberjack, a chargehand and a pawnbroker after I was a cartoonist which in turn was after I was a journalist and a signwriter. I was a signwriter before I was a pawnbroker, a pawnbroker before I was an upholsterer, an upholsterer before I was a programmer, a programmer before I was a fishmonger, a fishmonger before I was a piano-tuner and a chargehand, a chargehand before I was a blacksmith, and a blacksmith before I was a gamekeeper, an escapologist, a compositor and a piano-tuner. I was a piano-tuner before I was a lumberjack but that was after I had been a chargehand and an escapologist. I was also a greengrocer after being an upholsterer and an illustrator. Then again, I can also re-member being a greengrocer after I was an escapologist but before I was a piano-tuner.

'At one time I was a postmaster but that was before I was a pawnbroker, a chargehand and a newscaster which in turn was after I was an illustrator. I had quite a few jobs after I was an illustrator, including being a blacksmith, a gamekeeper, a newscaster, an escapologist and a program-mer. One thing that I do know is that I haven't done the same type of job twice. As I said before, I liked my job as a woodcarver but that was before I was a taxi-driver, an interpreter, a compositor, a gamekeeper and an electrician. I was actually an electrician before I was a gamekeeper.

'One job that I wasn't too keen on was that time I was an upholsterer, but that was before I was a ringmaster, a newscaster, a blacksmith and a compositor. I was a com-positor after I was a chargehand and a lumberjack. One quite boring job was that of a programmer which was after I was a newscaster and a ringmaster, and I was a ringmaster before I was a newscaster. The only other things I can remember is that I was a chargehand after I was a fishmon-ger and a pawnbroker, and that I was a pawnbroker before I was a fishmonger.'

Given what Jack said, see if you can make a list of the jobs he has had since being a journalist and the order in which he has had them.

Q63 Odd One Out★★★ A4

The diagrams below are that of a flattened cube and three views of the cube before it was flattened. Which of the three views is incorrect? (The cube can be restored to its original form by folding along the dotted lines.)

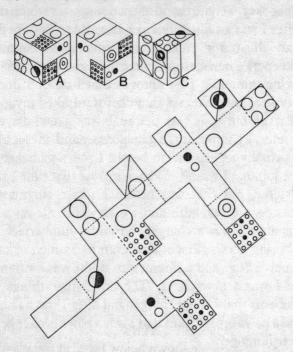

Q64 Wordsquares★ A32

Fit the 16 words into the four grids to form four word-squares which read the same down and across.

AGAR DOTE EDGE ELSE ENOW HOME IDEA LIMP

MEAL MEMO MERE OPEN ORAL PALE TASS TEAM

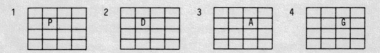

Q65 Blocked★★★ A73

Each of the 25 blocks of four letters shown below can be rotated about its centre, either 90° clockwise, 90° anticlockwise or 180°. When all of the 25 blocks are in their correct positions, all ten rows and columns contain the letters A to J only once.

Thirteen of the blocks shown below are not in their correct positions. Given that each of the five rows and columns of blocks contains at least one and no more than four blocks which have been rotated, which 13 of the 25 have been rotated and in which direction(s)?

	A	B	C	D	E
1	H J / B H	F D / C A	F I / E B	D G / A I	J C / E G
2	A G / F E	J I / G D	C H / A C	F E / I B	J H / B D
3	G D / E B	F H / I B	J G / A J	C D / E C	H F / A I
4	C I / I F	A J / C E	H D / D B	H B / J G	F E / G A
5	A D / C J	G B / E H	F E / I G	F J / H A	C I / B D

Q66 Piano Lessons★ A108

Complete the timetable shown below for next week's piano lessons, using the following information.

1. Brian has a grade one lesson on Monday and Tuesday.
2. Susan does not have a lesson on Wednesday or Thursday.
3. Tommy has a lesson on Thursday.
4. There are no grade one, three or five lessons on Friday.
5. Both Susan and Lucy have two lessons next week.
6. Julie has a grade three lesson the day after Jill has a grade five lesson which is not on Monday.
7. There are no grade one or grade three lessons on Wednesday.

continued overleaf

8. Susan has a grade two lesson in the afternoon of the same day in which Lucy has a grade four lesson.
9. There is a grade three lesson on Thursday afternoon and a grade one lesson on Thursday morning.
10. There are no grade five lessons on an afternoon.
11. John has a grade three lesson in the afternoon of the day before Susan has her grade two lesson.
12. No-one has two lessons on the same day.

	MORNING		AFTERNOON	
	NAME	GRADE	NAME	GRADE
MONDAY				
TUESDAY				
WEDNESDAY				
THURSDAY				
FRIDAY				

Q67   Mix Up Squared*   A45

Complete the square so that all of the columns and rows contain the letters:

S   Q   U   A   R   E   D

Each of the seven letters must only appear once in each column or row.

S	Q	U	A	R	E	D
	A				G	
D		Q	R			
			E			
	E	R	Q			
E						S
		A			S	R

Q68 Logic Box* A118

Using the following clues, place the letters A to I inclusive
into the grid. A is below B which is to the right of H and
above C which is to the left of G which is below E and above
F which is to the right of I. ('Above/below' refers to two
letters in the same column. 'Left of/right of' refers to two
letters in the same row.)

Q69 Clockwork*** A22

Diagram One is that of the numbers 1, 2, 3 and 4, each of
which is surrounded by eight circles, all of which contain a
different letter. The eight circles around each of the four
numbers can be rotated either 90° clockwise, 90° anticlockwise or 180°. For example, if 1 were to be rotated 90°
clockwise, the letter A would replace the letter F, D would
replace G, F would replace H, G would replace E, H would
replace C, etc.

Diagram Two is that of Diagram One after seven rotations of the letters around the four numbers—two clockwise, two anticlockwise and three through 180°. The letters
around each number have been rotated at least once but no
more than twice. In what order, and in what direction, have
the letters around each number been rotated in Diagram
One to arrive at the positions shown in Diagram Two?

Diagram One

Ⓐ Ⓓ Ⓕ Ⓘ Ⓚ Ⓝ Ⓟ Ⓢ Ⓤ
Ⓑ ① Ⓖ ② Ⓛ ③ Ⓠ ④ Ⓥ
Ⓒ Ⓔ Ⓗ Ⓙ Ⓜ Ⓞ Ⓡ Ⓣ Ⓦ

Diagram Two

Ⓗ Ⓔ Ⓟ Ⓢ Ⓚ Ⓘ Ⓒ Ⓞ Ⓤ
Ⓖ ① Ⓙ ② Ⓝ ③ Ⓠ ④ Ⓥ
Ⓕ Ⓓ Ⓜ Ⓛ Ⓐ Ⓑ Ⓡ Ⓣ Ⓦ

Q70 Number Fill★ A14

Given that the same number does not appear in two adjacent squares, either vertically, horizontally or diagonally, fit the numbers 1 to 12 inclusive four times each into the grid below. Only one number should be entered into each square. Some of the numbers appear next to the row and/or beneath the column into which they should be placed.

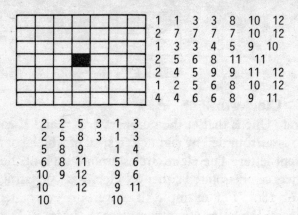

1	1	3	3	8	10	12
2	7	7	7	7	10	12
1	3	3	4	5	9	10
2	5	6	8	11	11	
2	4	5	9	9	11	12
1	2	5	6	8	10	12
4	4	6	6	8	9	11

2	2	5	3	1	3
2	5	8	3	1	3
5	8	9		1	4
6	8	11		5	6
10	9	12		9	6
10		12		9	11
10				10	

Q71 Consider★★ A56

Consider the following diagram:

Which of the following six diagrams is the odd one out?

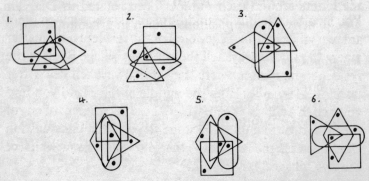

50

Q72   Grid Fill*** A5
Fit the 36 words into the grid below.

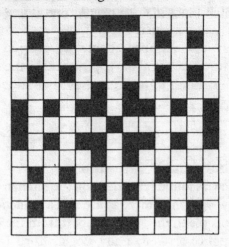

AGATE ALPHA   AROSE ATOLL CAMEL CHAIR

COMET COUCH   CRAZE DURRA EATEN ECLAT

ERODE ERROR   EXTRA HIPPO LADEN LUCRE

MANIC MANOR   NEVER OARED REEST REEVE

RENTE RIVET   SENSE SHRED SLEEP STEIN

THREE TOWEL   TROPE UREDO USAGE WORST

Q73   Somewhere* A136
You have been left in the middle of an island on which there are two villages. In village A, all of the residents, no matter where they are, always tell the truth. In village B, all of the residents, no matter where they are, always tell lies. After walking a few miles from the middle of the island you find yourself in a village square where there is a resident of one of the villages sitting on some stone steps. What one question would you ask the resident so that you would know which of the two villages you were in?

Q74 Square Cut★ A83

Divide the square into four parts of equal size and shape, each of which must include one A, one B and one C.

		A	A	A	
		B	B	C	C
	A		B		
				B	
C	C				

Q75 Whodunnit?★★★★ A96

Lord Logic was found lying dead on the kitchen floor. Next to the body was a hammer, a vase and a truncheon. There were four people in the kitchen, apart from the dead body, when the police arrived; Lady Logic, Lord Logic's mistress, the butler and the maid. There were five detectives working on the case, each of whom took a statement from all four suspects. Given that only 10 of the 20 statements given were true, who killed Lord Logic, and with what?

Detective	Suspect	Statement given by suspect
I	Butler	The maid killed Lord Logic with the hammer.
I	Maid	The butler killed Lord Logic with the vase.
I	Lady Logic	Lord Logic's mistress did not kill him with the hammer.
I	Mistress	I killed Lord Logic with the vase.
2	Butler	Lady Logic hit Lord Logic over the head with the hammer and killed him.
2	Maid	The butler killed Lord Logic using the truncheon.

2	Lady Logic	The butler killed Lord Logic using the vase.
2	Mistress	Lady Logic did not kill Lord Logic with the vase.
3	Butler	Lord Logic's mistress did not kill him with the vase.
3	Maid	Lady Logic used the vase to kill Lord Logic.
3	Lady Logic	My husband's mistress did not kill him with a truncheon.
3	Mistress	Lady Logic killed her husband by hitting him on the back of the head with the hammer.
4	Butler	Lord Logic was killed by his mistress. She hit him over the head with the truncheon.
4	Maid	Lady Logic did not kill her husband with the truncheon.
4	Lady Logic	The maid killed my husband with the vase.
4	Mistress	The butler did it, he killed Lord Logic with the truncheon.
5	Butler	The maid did not kill Lord Logic with the truncheon.
5	Maid	Lady Logic killed her husband with the hammer.
5	Lady Logic	I killed my husband with the hammer.
5	Mistress	The maid hit Lord Logic with the vase and killed him.

The reporter for the local *Gazette* was at the national dog show yesterday. Unfortunately he also had to report on quite a few other events on the same day. He made some notes when he was at the dog show which are shown below, but the editor of the *Gazette* has asked for a list of the 26 finalists and the positions in which they finished overall. Using the reporter's notes below, see if you can construct the list for the editor, as the reporter didn't have time to make a note of the overall positions.

The Afghan Hound finished before the Alsatian, the Poodle and the Beagle. The Beagle finished before the Bull Mastiff and the Labrador. The Labrador finished before the Poodle and the Pug. The Pug finished before the Alsatian, the Dobermann Pinscher, the St Bernard, the Sheepdog and the Griffon. The Griffon finished before the Sheepdog. The Sheepdog finished after the Poodle. The Poodle finished before the St Bernard, the Collie, the Pug, the Griffon, the Alsatian and the Dobermann Pinscher. The Dobermann Pinscher finished after the Alsatian. The Alsatian finished after the Chow. The Chow finished before the Afghan Hound, the Bulldog, the Chihuahua, the Poodle, the Beagle and the Dachshund. The Dachshund finished before the Spaniel. The Spaniel finished before the Foxhound.

The Foxhound finished before the Labrador. The Labrador finished after the Whippet. The Whippet finished before the Great Dane. The Great Dane finished after the Bull Terrier and before the Chow. The Chow finished before the Bull Mastiff. The Bull Mastiff finished before the Foxhound. The Foxhound finished after the Yorkshire Terrier. The Yorkshire Terrier finished before the Greyhound. The Greyhound finished before the Dachshund. The Dachshund finished after the King Charles Spaniel. The King Charles Spaniel finished before the Bull Mastiff, the Greyhound, the Pug, the Chihuahua and the

Afghan Hound. The Afghan Hound finished after the Dalmatian. The Dalmatian finished before the Pug, the Labrador, the Poodle and the Collie.

The Collie finished before the Pug. The Pug finished after the Retriever. The Retriever finished before the Bull Terrier, the Chow, the Yorkshire Terrier and the Whippet. The Whippet finished before the Chow, the Spaniel, the Dalmatian and the Yorkshire Terrier. The Yorkshire Terrier finished after the Bulldog. The Bulldog finished before the Chihuahua and the Dalmatian. The Dalmatian finished after the Great Dane. The Great Dane finished before the Yorkshire Terrier. The Yorkshire Terrier finished before the Collie, the King Charles Spaniel, the Spaniel and the Dalmatian. The Dalmatian finished after the Spaniel. The Griffon finished before the Alsatian. The Alsatian finished after the Sheepdog. The Griffon finished after the St Bernard. The Greyhound finished before the Chihuahua. The Chihuahua finished before the Dachshund. The Bull Terrier finished before the Whippet and the Yorkshire Terrier. The Afghan Hound finished before the Pug and the Foxhound.

Q77 Odd Block Out★ A97
Which is the odd block out?

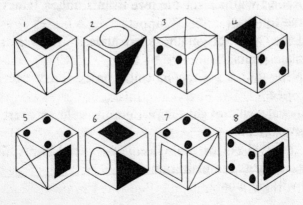

1. Tracey will not get the chocolate-covered mints unless Neil has the plain mints.

2. Alan will not get the toffee unless Robert has the mint-flavoured toffee.

3. Neil will not get the plain mints unless Alan has the mint-flavoured toffee.

4. Robert will not get the toffee unless Tracey gets the plain mints.

5. Robert will not get the chocolate-covered mints unless Tracey gets the toffee.

6. Tracey will not get the toffee unless Neil gets the chocolate.

7. Robert will not get the mint-flavoured toffee unless James gets the plain mints.

8. Alan will not get the plain mints unless Tracey gets the toffee.

9. Tracey will not get the plain mints unless Alan gets the chocolate-covered mints.

10. Alan will not get the mint-flavoured toffee unless Tracey gets the chocolate-covered mints.

11. James will not get the plain mints unless Tracey gets the toffee.

12. Neil will not get the chocolate unless Alan gets the chocolate-covered mints.

13. Robert will not get the plain mints unless James gets the toffee.

14. James will not get the toffee unless Tracey gets the plain mints.

15. Neil will not get the chocolate unless Tracey gets the toffee.

16. Tracey will not get the plain mints unless Robert gets the toffee.

17. Alan will not get the chocolate-covered mints unless James gets the plain mints.

Who will get what?

Q79 Odd One Out*** A129

The diagrams below are that of a flattened cube and three views of the cube before it was flattened. Which of the three views is incorrect? (The cube can be restored to its original form by folding along the dotted lines.)

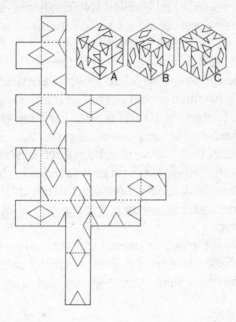

Q80 Logic Box* A65

Using the following clues, place the letters A to I inclusive into the grid. C is below D which is to the left of H and to the right of B which is to the left of H which is above E and A. F is to the right of G which is below I which is to the left of E. ('Above/below' refers to two letters in the same column. 'Left of/right of' refers to two letters in the same row.)

Q81   Boxed**   A119

There are four boxes on a shelf, all in a straight horizontal line. Each box contains a pair of gloves and a scarf. No box contains a pair of gloves and scarf the same colour as the box or each other. All four boxes, pairs of gloves and scarves are either red, green, blue or yellow. No two boxes are the same colour, no two scarves are the same colour and no two pairs of gloves are the same colour.

The red scarf is in the box next to the box containing the pair of green gloves. The yellow gloves are in the box next to the green box which is next to the box containing the green scarf. The box on the far left is red. The blue gloves are in the box next to the box containing the blue scarf. The yellow box isn't next to the blue box which is next to the box containing the red gloves. The green scarf is in the blue box or the yellow box. The yellow scarf is not in the red box which is not, and is not next to, the box containing the yellow gloves.

From the information given, see if you can determine the position of each box on the shelf, what the colour of each box is, and the colour of the gloves and scarf each box contains.

Q82   Wordsquares*   A84

Fit the 16 words into the four grids to form four word-squares which read the same down and across.

AGED   AMEN   AREA   DAME   DEMO   EARN   EDEN   ENOW

ERNE   MADE   MANE   MERE   MORE   NEAR   NEED   OMEN

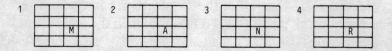

Q83 Letter Boxes* A142

When the diagram below is complete, each column and row and one of the diagonals should contain the letters A, B, C, D, E, F, G, H, I and J. See if you can complete the diagram by fitting the eight blocks of nine letters into the eight highlighted squares and filling in the remaining spaces.

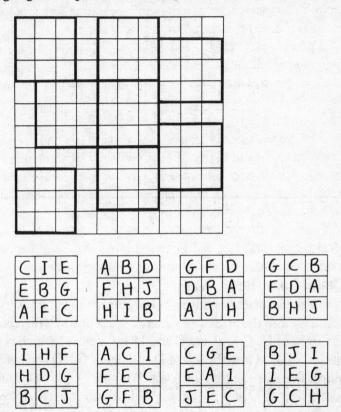

Q84 Blocked*** A54

Each of the 25 blocks of four letters shown on page 60 can be rotated about its centre, either 90° clockwise or 90° anti-clockwise. When all of the 25 blocks are in their correct positions, all ten rows and columns contain the letters A to J only once.

continued overleaf

Twenty of the blocks shown below are not in their correct positions. Given that each of the five rows and columns of blocks contain one block which has not been rotated, ten blocks have been rotated clockwise and ten blocks have been rotated anticlockwise, which 20 of the 25 have been rotated and in which direction?

	A	B	C	D	E
1	A F / G H	C B / E C	H D / A G	D J / J F	I B / E I
2	D G / F I	H A / I J	G C / H J	E B / B E	C F / D A
3	C H / I J	D J / G E	B E / C F	A G / I H	B F / A D
4	D B / A C	I F / F A	I J / E B	H C / D G	E H / G J
5	E B / J E	D G / H B	D F / I A	I C / F A	G C / J H

Q85 Logic Box★ A27

Using the information given below, place the letters A to P inclusive into the grid of 16 squares. L is above J which is to the right of H. O is above C and H and below I which is to the left of B. M is to the left of D and below G. N is below E, above D and to the right of A which is above G, below P and to the right of O and F. ('Above/below' refers to two letters in the same column. 'Left of/right of' refers to two letters in the same row.)

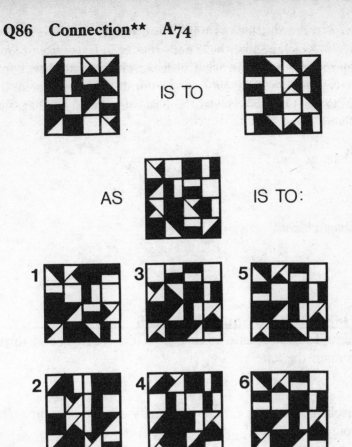

IS TO

AS   IS TO:

1   3   5

2   4   6

Q87 Clockwork*** A15

Diagram One is that of the numbers 1, 2, 3 and 4, each of which is surrounded by eight circles, all of which contain a different letter. The eight circles around each of the four numbers can be rotated either 90° clockwise, 90° anticlockwise or 180°. For example, if 1 were to be rotated 90° clockwise, the letter A would replace the letter F, D would replace G, F would replace H, G would replace E, H would replace C, etc.

Diagram Two is that of Diagram One after seven rotations of the letters around the four numbers – three clockwise, three anticlockwise and one through 180°. The letters around each number have been rotated at least once but no more than twice. In what order, and in which direction, have the letters around each number been rotated in Diagram One to arrive at the positions shown in Diagram Two?

Diagram One
Ⓐ Ⓓ Ⓕ Ⓘ Ⓚ Ⓝ Ⓟ Ⓢ Ⓤ
Ⓑ ① Ⓖ ② Ⓛ ③ Ⓠ ④ Ⓥ
Ⓒ Ⓔ Ⓗ Ⓙ Ⓜ Ⓞ Ⓡ Ⓣ Ⓦ

Diagram Two
Ⓒ Ⓑ Ⓗ Ⓖ Ⓜ Ⓛ Ⓦ Ⓣ Ⓡ
Ⓔ ① Ⓝ ② Ⓞ ③ Ⓥ ④ Ⓠ
Ⓚ Ⓙ Ⓥ Ⓘ Ⓟ Ⓢ Ⓕ Ⓖ Ⓐ

Q88 Mix Up Squarely★ A46

Complete the square so that all of the columns and rows contain the letters:

 S   Q   U   A   R   E   L   Y

Each of the eight letters must only appear once in each column or row.

S	Q	U	A	R	E	L	Y
R	L		E				S
					Y		E
	R	E			S	U	
Y			L	S		Q	U
	A		Q				
				Q	U	S	
A			S			Y	L

62

Q89 Laser Maze*** A6

The diagram below represents an aerial view of a room which has been divided into 100 squares, as shown by the dotted lines. In each of the squares there should be a dot marked on the floor of the centre of the square, or a double-sided mirror. When all of the dots and mirrors are in their correct places, a laser beam can enter the room at square A1 in the direction indicated by an arrow, and leave the room from square J10. At the same time, the laser beam shines over each and every dot marked on the floor. When the beam reaches a mirror it 'bounces off' at an angle of 90°, but it never crosses itself. If the beam hits the outside wall it is absorbed by the wall and can go no further.

Sixteen of the dots/mirrors are not in place: three dots (X), five mirrors from lower left to upper right (Y), and eight mirrors from upper left to lower right (Z). See if you can determine which of the squares containing '?' should be replaced by:

1. X squares.   2. Y squares.   3. Z squares.

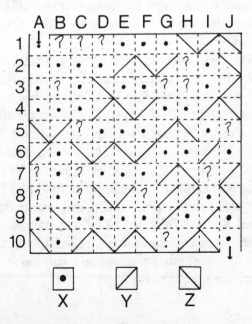

Q90 What Colour Next?***** A55

My next-door neighbour paints his garden fence a different colour every two weeks. Last year he painted his fence 26 different colours. Given the following information, in what order, colourwise, did my neighbour paint his fence last year?

He painted the fence Coal Black before he painted it Ruby Red, Pitch Black, Yellow, Oxford Blue and Creamy White. The fence was painted Jade Green before it was painted Pitch Black and Oxford Blue but was painted Jade Green after it was painted Navy Blue, Hazel Brown, Creamy White and Yellow. It was painted Yellow before it was painted Mauve but after it was painted Lavender.

My neighbour painted the fence Lavender before he painted it Coal Black, Ruby Red, Olive Green, Lemon, Pitch Black, Yellow and Mauve. He painted the fence Mauve after he painted it White but before he painted it Creamy White. In turn, he painted the fence Creamy White after he painted it Violet and after he painted it Sky Blue, but he painted it Sky Blue before he painted it Hazel Brown which was after he painted it Navy Blue, Olive green, Indigo and Violet.

The fence was painted Violet before it was Turquoise, Turquoise before it was Emerald Green, Emerald Green before it was Sky Blue, Sky Blue after it was Navy Blue, Navy Blue before it was Lavender, Lavender after it was Orange, Orange before it was Burgundy, and Burgundy before it was Navy Blue. He painted it Sea Blue before he painted it Purple which in turn was before he painted it Ruby Red and Primrose. The fence was painted Ruby Red before it was painted Red, and it was also painted Pitch Black and Oxford Blue before it was painted Red. He painted the fence Oxford Blue before painting it Ruby Red, Sea Blue, Purple and Primrose and painted it Primrose before painting it Ruby Red.

My neighbour painted his fence Orange before he painted it Oxford Blue, Violet and Navy Blue, but he painted it Navy Blue before he painted it Indigo and Violet, and Violet after he painted it Olive Green, Indigo and Burgundy. The fence was painted Fawn before it was painted Oxford Blue, but was painted Fawn after being painted Hazel Brown, Violet and Pitch Black.

The fence was painted Pitch Black before it was painted Sea Blue, Oxford Blue, Purple, Primrose and Ruby Red, but was painted Pitch Black after it was painted Hazel Brown which was before it was painted Oxford Blue and Coal Black. My neighbour painted the fence White before he painted it Emerald Green, Emerald Green after he painted it Lemon, and Lemon after he had painted it Olive Green, Turquoise and White, and White after he had painted it Violet but before he had painted it Turquoise, Coal Black and Oxford Blue. Also, the fence was painted Violet before it was painted Sky Blue, Burgundy before it was painted Indigo, and Indigo before it was painted Lavender.

Q91   Coin Puzzle★   A98
Using twelve coins, create a square which has five coins along each side.

Q92 Father Unlike Son★ A33

There is one grandfather, one father (not counting the grandfather) and one son (not counting the father) in each of the Smith, Jones and Brown families. Each of the nine is either a plumber, a joiner or a bricklayer. Grandfather Smith is a joiner and no-one with the surname Jones has a son or grandson who is a bricklayer, but someone with the surname Brown has a father who is a bricklayer. Also, no-one has the same occupation as his father, grandfather, son or grandson. Given that no two grandfathers, fathers or sons have the same occupation, what is the occupation of the Jones son who isn't a father?

Q93 Odd One Out★★★ A16

The diagrams below are that of a flattened cube and three views of the cube before it was flattened. Which of the three views is incorrect? (The cube can be restored to its original form by folding along the dotted lines.)

Q94 Grid Fill*** A130
Fit the 36 words into the grid below.

AXIAL CLOTH CURIO DOMED DRAMA EGRET

ELOIN ENACT FIGHT FORME FRONT GIANT

HODGE HORDE INFRA IRADE KNEEL LARGE

LILAC MOODY NAMER OFFAL OIDIA OLDIE

ORACH ORATE OSTIA PATCH PEDAL RATEL

ROTOR TEHEE TIMER TITLE WAFER WHELK

Q95 Square Cut* A75
Divide the square into four parts of equal size and shape,
each of which must include the letters A to P inclusive.

M	C	K	E	M	K	I	J
I	I	O	E	L	B	G	G
N	K	J	E	H	B	H	L
P	B	G	A	A	D	P	E
F	J	B	A	A	D	N	G
F	N	D	I	F	D	O	N
P	F	H	C	O	L	C	P
O	M	H	C	L	J	K	M

Given that the same number does not appear in two adjacent squares, either vertically, horizontally or diagonally, fit the numbers 1 to 15 inclusive four times each into the grid below. Only one number should be entered into each square. Some of the numbers appear next to the row and/or beneath the column into which they should be placed.

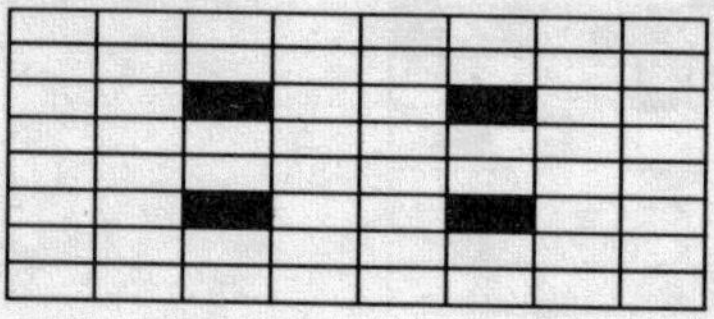

Numbers beside the rows:

1	3	8	8	9	11	12	15
1	2	5	5	6	6	6	14
8	11	11	12	12	12		
1	2	5	6	7	7	7	14
1	2	3	8	9	9	13	13
4	7	10	10	11	15		
2	3	3	5	9	13	13	14
4	4	4	10	10	14	15	15

Numbers beneath the columns:

1	3	2	11	2	2	7	6
1		5	11	6	2	7	6
6		5	11	8	3	8	10
10		5		8	3	8	10
10		15		12	3	9	12
12		15		14	4	9	12
13				15			13
13				15			13

Q97 Cross Check** A23

Look along each line horizontally, and then look down each line vertically, to find the missing square.

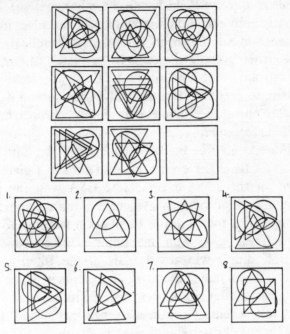

Q98 Logicalympics – Swimming*** A47

Four countries entered the logicalympics swimming events: Great Britain (GB), Germany (G), the United States of America (USA) and China (C). There were eight events in all: 100m freestyle, 100m backstroke, 100m breaststroke, 100m butterfly, 200m freestyle, 200m backstroke, 200m breaststroke and 200m butterfly. All four countries entered three swimmers in each of the eight events. In true logicalympic style, there was no overall winner; each of the four countries won two gold medals, two silver medals and two bronze medals. Given the following information, see if you can work out which country won the gold medal, silver medal and bronze medal in each event.

continued overleaf

The USA didn't win any 200m event and won no medals at all in any butterfly event. GB won one 100m event and one 200m event. C was the only country to win all three medals in one event. G won only one medal out of both butterfly events, and did not win a gold and silver medal in the same event. GB won a total of two medals in the breaststroke events. G won a silver medal in one of the breaststroke events and won a total of two medals in the backstroke events. GB won a silver medal and a bronze medal in one of the 100m events. C won a bronze medal in the 100m freestyle.

GB won only one bronze medal out of the four bronze medals for the 200m events, and did not win a silver medal in any of the 200m events. The USA won the bronze medal in both of the events where GB won the gold medal. C won a silver medal in the 100m event won by GB which wasn't freestyle. G won one 100m event and one 200m event. C didn't win any medals in the 100m butterfly event. GB won one of the two 200m events in which G won no medals at all. C didn't win a single medal in any of the backstroke events. G won a bronze medal and a silver medal in one of the 100m events.

Q99   What Next?*   A57
Find the next most appropriate pentagon.

Choose from:

Q100 Odd One Out★ A110
Which one of the following ten diagrams is the odd one out?

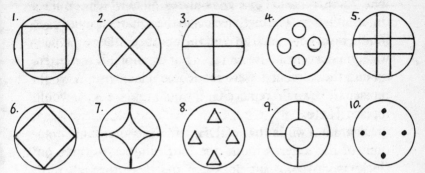

Q101 Logic Box★ A99
Using the information given below, place the letters A to P inclusive into the grid of 16 squares.

A is below I, which is to the left of C.
B is below O and to the left of C.
E is below H, which is to the left of A.
G is below F and to the left of B and C.
J is above M and to the right of H.
L is below K.
M is to the left of L.
N is above C and K.
O is to the left of D.
P is to the right of M.

('Above/below' refers to two letters in the same column. 'Left of/right of' refers to two letters in the same row.)

Q102 Clockwork Links**** A120

Diagram One is that of the numbers 1, 2, 3 and 4, each of which is surrounded by eight squares, all of which contain a different letter. The eight letters in the squares around each number can be rotated around the number either 90° clockwise, 90° anticlockwise or 180°. For example, if the letters around the number 1 were rotated 90° clockwise, A would replace C, B would replace G, C would replace K, G would replace J, etc.

Diagram Two is that of Diagram One after eight rotations of the letters around the four numbers – three 90° clockwise, two 90° anticlockwise and three through 180°. The letters have been rotated twice around each number. In what order, and in which direction have the letters been rotated around each number to arrive at the positions shown in Diagram Two?

Diagram One

A	B	C	D	E
F	**1**	G	**2**	H
I	J	K	L	M
N	**3**	O	**4**	P
Q	R	S	T	U

Diagram Two

Q	D	A	N	K
F	**1**	R	**2**	L
E	H	M	B	C
J	**3**	G	**4**	T
I	P	U	O	S

Q103 Post Problem* A86

The diagram below represents a square courtyard containing nine wooden posts. I have two sets of fencing, each of which can form a square of any size. Using the two sets of fencing, is it possible to divide the courtyard into nine separate sections with one post in each section? If so, how?

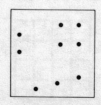

72

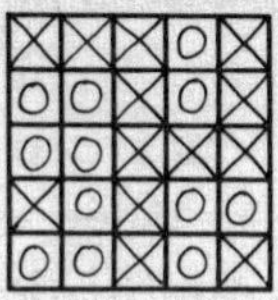

IS TO

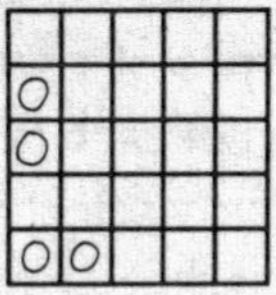

AS 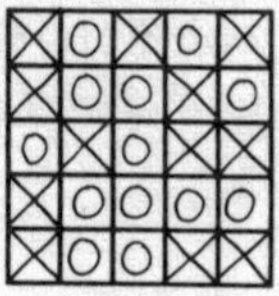   IS TO:

1 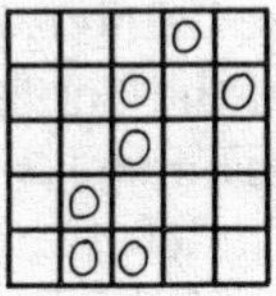   3 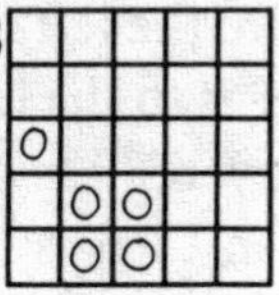   5 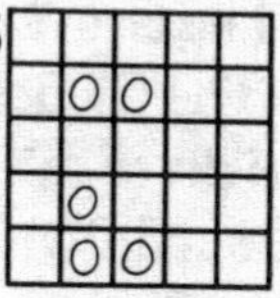   7

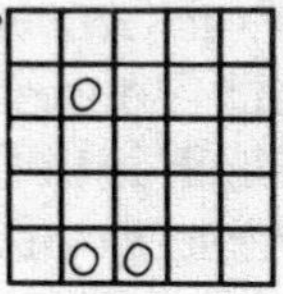

2 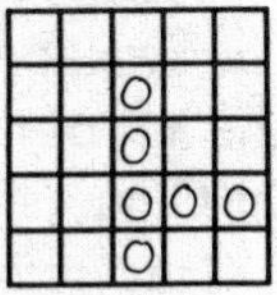   4 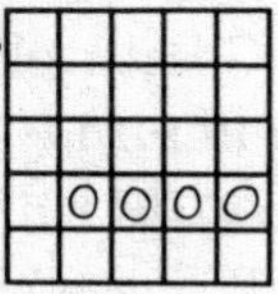   6 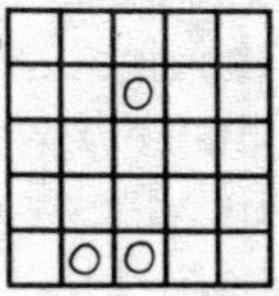   8

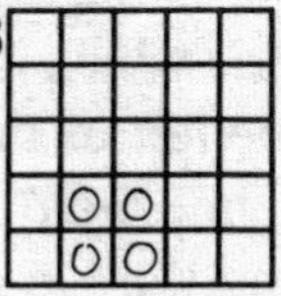

One of the local supermarkets has a special cheese counter where various types of cheese are all laid out in a straight line. The position of each type of cheese is never changed so that you can quickly select your choice of cheese when you visit the supermarket. From the following information, make a list of the cheeses in the order in which they are arranged on the supermarket counter, starting from the left-hand side and assuming you are facing the cheese counter.

The Stilton is to the left of the Mycella which is to the right of the Gruyère. The Gruyère is to the left of the Gambozola and Gloucester. The Gloucester is to the left of the Cottage which is to the right of the Gruyère. The Camembert is to the left of the Boursin which in turn is to the left of the Westminster Blue. The Westminster Blue is to the right of the Cottage as is the Boursin. The Gouda is to the left of the Brie which is to the right of the Gorgonzola. The Swiss is to the left of the Cotswold which in turn is to the left of the Lymeswold. The Lymeswold is to the left of the Gloucester and the Camembert. The Gorgonzola and the Gruyère are to the right of the Camembert.

   The Tilsiter is to the left of the Pecorino which in turn is to the left of the Port Salut. The Port Salut is to the left of the Parmesan and the Wensleydale. The Wensleydale is to the left of the Gouda which is to the right of the Jarlsberg. The Jarlsberg is to the left of the Cheshire which in turn is to the left of the Swiss. The Swiss is to the right of the Port Salut which is to the left of the Camembert and the Brickbat. The Brickbat is to the left of the Swiss. The Roquefort is also to the left of the Swiss.

   The Gorgonzola is to the left of the Wensleydale which is to the right of the Roquefort which in turn is to the left of the Cheshire. The Cheshire is to the left of the Brickbat which is to the right of the Parmesan. The Parmesan is to the left of the Jarlsberg which in turn is to the left of the Lymeswold. The Lymeswold is to the left of the Cottage which in turn is to the left of the Gambozola. The Gambozola is to the left of the Stilton which in turn is to the left of the Boursin and to the right of the Cottage.

The Cottage is to the left of the Mycella which in turn is to the left of the Boursin. The Boursin is to the right of the Port Salut as is the Gorgonzola. The Parmesan is to the left of the Lymeswold which is to the right of the Percorino which in turn is to the left of the Jarlsberg and to the right of the Edam. The Edam is to the left of the Tilsiter which in turn is to the left of the Brie. The Brie is to the left of the Gruyère which is to the right of the Port Salut.

The Port Salut is to the right of the Tilsiter and the Cheddar. The Cheddar is to the left of the Tilsiter. The Edam is to the left of the Jarlsberg and to the right of the Cheddar. The Cheddar is to the left of the Cottage. The Brie is also to the left of the Cottage. The Lymeswold is to the left of the Brie and the Gruyère which in turn is to the left of the Westminster Blue. The Brickbat and the Camembert are to the right of the Roquefort which is to the left of the Cottage.

The Cottage is to the right of the Camembert which is to the left of the Gouda. The Gouda is to the right of the Cotswold which in turn is to the right of the Tilsiter and the Jarlsberg. The Jarlsberg is to the left of the Gloucester and the Roquefort and is to the right of the Tilsiter and the Cheddar. The Tilsiter is to the left of the Lymeswold. The Stilton is to the right of the Gambozola and the Gruyère which in turn is to the left of the Boursin.

Q106 Mix Up Squarebox* A39

Complete the square so that all of the columns and rows contain the letters:

S Q U A R E B O X

Each of the nine letters must only appear once in each column or row.

B	S			Q				X
	E	X			B	R	O	
		Q	E	X		B	S	
		A	X		E	U	B	
	O	B		R				
X			A		S			O
		U		S		O		
	Q		O	E		S	U	
S		B			Q		X	A

Q107 Sparky*** A66

Eddie the electrician has eight different jobs to complete today, all of which are at different times and at different houses in Bright Street. Eddie's secretary, who isn't organised at all, has left a list of jumbled notes about the jobs that have to be completed in Bright Street. Using these notes, see if you can construct a timetable for Eddie so that he knows which job needs completing at each house and the time he has to be there.

Notes

Mend dishwasher at No. 51. Mend fridge motor at 11.00am. Go to No. 31 at 4.00pm. You have a 10.00am appointment at Bright Street. Don't go to No. 13 first or last. Go to No. 27 before installing cooker point at No. 14. Install alcove light after mending dishwasher. Mend the vacuum cleaner before the fridge motor. Your last job is at 5.00pm and your first at 9.00am. Mend the electric shower at 3.00pm. Go to No. 2 before Nos. 14 and 9 and after 51. Install the cooker point before mending the electric shower but not after lunch. Do not mend the dishwasher first. Mend the broken socket after the electric shower. Install the wall lights at No. 43 after installing the alcove light at No. 9. You have a 2.00pm and a 12noon appointment in Bright Street.

Q108 Letter Boxes*** A141

When the diagram below is complete, each column and row should contain the letters A, B, C, D, E, F, G, H, I and J. See if you can complete the diagram by fitting the seven blocks of nine letters into the seven highlighted squares and filling in the remaining squares.

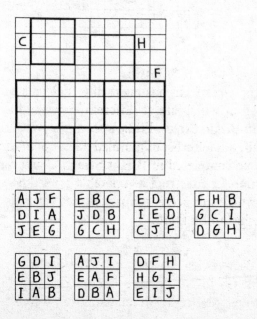

Each of the 25 blocks of four letters shown below can be rotated about its centre, either 90° clockwise, 90° anticlockwise or 180°. When all of the 25 blocks are in their correct positions, all ten rows and columns contain the letters A to J only once.

Fourteen of the blocks shown below are not in their correct positions. Given that five blocks have been rotated clockwise and five blocks have been rotated anticlockwise, which 14 of the 25 have been rotated and in which direction?

	A	B	C	D	E
1	C J / B A	H J / G B	I D / E I	A G / D F	H C / F E
2	G F / C E	H F / D I	B C / A G	J I / B E	J A / H D
3	A I / D J	C I / F G	J C / H G	A H / B E	D F / B E
4	E H / I G	J E / B A	A D / F H	C D / F C	B I / G J
5	F H / D B	A E / C D	J B / E F	J H / I G	C G / A I

Q110 Odd One Out***** A76

The diagrams below are that of a flattened cube and three views of the cube before it was flattened. Which of the three views is incorrect? This time only two of the dotted lines along which the original cube was folded are shown.

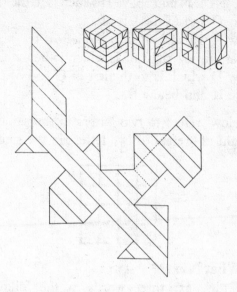

Q111 Odd Block Out*** A100

Which is the odd block out?

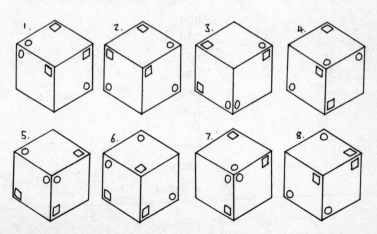

Q112 Logic Box★ A121

Using the information given below, place the letters A to P inclusive into the grid of 16 squares.

I is to the right of H and below B.
C is to the left of N and above H which is to the right of P.
P is below O and to the left of I.
M is below A which is also to the left of I.
K and F are to the right of L which is below G.
J is below D which is to the left of G and M.
E is above K and below B.

('Above/below' refers to two letters in the same column. 'Left of/right of' refers to two letters in the same row.)

Q113 What Next?★ A111

What are the next three words in the following list? (Remember, there are no mathematics involved!)

one
seven
one
two
six
four
two
five
three
seven
four
———
———
———

Q114 Nine By Four*** A87
Complete the grid using the following information.

Each of the 36 squares in the grid is filled with a single-digit number from 1 to 9, each of those numbers being used four times. The same number must not appear in two touching squares, either across, down or diagonally. Column E does not contain a 4. Row one contains two 9s. Square B2 contains the number 8. Column F contains one 5, one 7 and one 8. Square F3 contains the number 1. Squares B3 and C5 contain the number 2. Column D does not contain two of any number. Square D2 contains the number 1. Column F contains two 3s. Row six contains three 5s, one 9 and one 7. Column C contains two 4s, one 6, one 1 and one 8. Square E5 contains the number 6. Row three contains one 5. Column D does not contain an 8 or a 9. Column A contains three 9s. Row two contains one 3, two 6s and two 8s. Column B does not contain two of any number. Row four contains two 1s, two 7s, one 6 and one 2.

Q115 Chessboard* A17
Consider the following grid of letters.

Now, complete the grid below:

Q116 Block Cut* A28

Divide the rectangular block into four parts of equal size and shape. Each part should have the numbers 1 to 9 inclusive on the front, and all four new parts should form a square block when pieced together with all 36 numbers remaining the same way up.

Q117 Blocked*** A8

Each of the 25 blocks of four letters shown below can be rotated about its centre, either 90° clockwise, 90° anticlockwise or 180°. When all of the 25 blocks are in their correct positions, all ten rows and columns contain the letters A to J only once.

Sixteen of the blocks shown below are not in their correct positions. Which 16 of the 25 have been rotated and in which directions(s)?

	A	B	C	D	E
1	C D / B H	I H / A G	E G / J C	F B / O F	E I / A J
2	A E / I G	B G / C F	H J / F I	H E / A O	C B / D J
3	G I / A D	F D / B E	B E / C G	H J / J I	H F / A C
4	E F / F H	I J / J H	B A / A D	C G / G C	O E / I B
5	J B / C J	C D / E A	F D / H I	B A / I E	H G / G F

Q118   Grid Fill***   A34

Fit the 36 words into the grid below.

ABIDE   ADDLE   ADMIT   AFRIT   ALPHA   APHID

ASPIC   BENDY   CACHE   DENIM   EJECT   ELECT

ENACT   GUTSY   HADJI   HASTE   HEAVY   HEDGE

INTRO   LIVID   MITRE   NOMAD   PSALM   RAYED

RIANT   SCATT   SODIC   STUNG   TIPSY   TROUT

UDDER   UNMAN   UNRIP   URBAN   VICAR   YACHT

Q119   Logic Box*   A58

Using the information given below, place the letters A to P inclusive into the grid of 16 squares.

H is to the right of A which is to the left of N which is below B which is below L which is above C which is to the right of P which is to the right of J which is to the left of C which is to the right of F which is above K which is to the right of I which is above M which is below J which is below D which is to the left of O which is to the left of E which is above K which is to the right of G which is above A which is below P which is below O which is above G which is to the right of I.

('Above/below' refers to two letters in the same column. 'Left of/right of' refers to two letters in the same row.)

Q120 Odd One Out***** A101

The diagrams below are that of a flattened cube and three views of the cube before it was flattened. Which of the three views is incorrect? (This time only two of the dotted lines along which the original cube was folded are shown.)

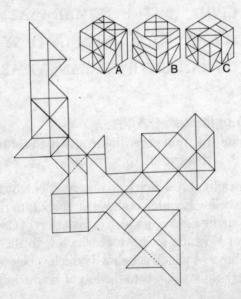

Q121   Clockwork Links****   A132

Diagram One is that of the numbers 1, 2, 3 and 4, each of which is surrounded by eight squares, all of which contain a different letter. The eight letters in the squares around each number can be rotated around the number either 90° clockwise, 90° anticlockwise or 180°. For example, if the letters around the number 1 were rotated 90° clockwise, A would replace C, B would replace G, C would replace K, G would replace J, etc.

Diagram Two is that of Diagram One after eight rotations of the letters around the four numbers – three 90° clockwise, two 90° anticlockwise and three through 180°. The letters have been rotated twice around each number. In what order, and in which direction, have the letters been rotated around each number to arrive at the positions shown in Diagram Two?

Diagram One		*Diagram Two*	

Diagram One

A	B	C	D	E
F	**1**	G	**2**	H
I	J	K	L	M
N	**3**	O	**4**	P
Q	R	S	T	U

Diagram Two

K	N	Q	D	E
T	**1**	J	**2**	H
I	G	A	B	C
F	**3**	O	**4**	P
U	R	M	L	S

Q122   Odd One Out**   A24

Which of the five numbered figures is the odd one out?

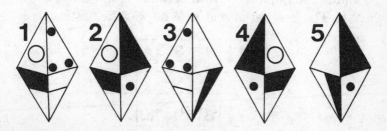

85

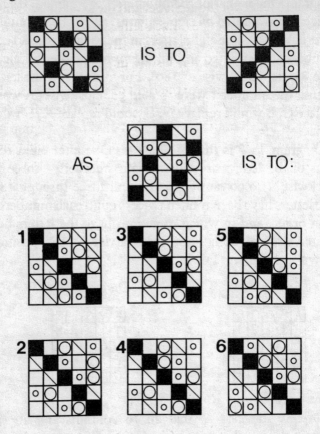

A sat opposite G who was sitting next to C. C sat opposite F. D sat between F and H, but not in seat 8 or 9. E sat between G and A and opposite J. I sat between B and C but not in seat 9. The host sat in seat 5. Who was the host?

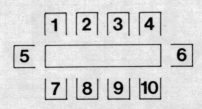

Q125 Logic Cube**** A77

Fit the 26 letters of the alphabet and the symbol '@' into the cube of 27 smaller cubes. Each letter is to be fitted into one of the smaller cubes, as is the '@'. Remember that some of the smaller cubes are not visible in the diagram below.

Y is behind R which is to the right of F. A is above T which in turn is above H. Y is in front of H. O is to the left of F and below B, which in turn is to the left of W. Q is behind N, E is behind V, P is behind @, J is behind Z, and I is behind L. S is above M and to the right of J, which in turn is above C. D is below L and to the right of N. W is above U, U is in front of M, and M is above P. V is to the left of @, G is to the left of X, and K is in front of S.

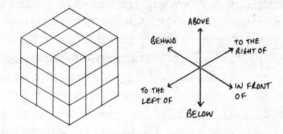

Q126 Mix Up 16*** A112

Complete the grid so that all 16 columns and 16 rows contain the numbers 1 to 16 inclusive. When complete, the grid reads the same down as across.

1	2	3	4	5	6	7	8	9	10	11	12	13	14	15	16
2	6								4		11		3	16	12
3	9	12			5							16			7
4			15					11			16	1	14	3	
5						13			16					11	15
6	5	8			2	1		14		16	15			12	11
7	10					15	2		16	3	14	11	6	9	8
8	14			9			16		7			11	10	4	
9	8			1	16	15		13		5					10
10				16	6	2				15					14
11	15	4	8	12	16			9	6			10			1
12			16				3		1						5
13	7		16		10		1		14	8		2			9
14		16			9			12			7		15	13	
15	16	13						7		5		3			2
16															

Q127 Birthday Boys*** A18

Eddie has bought a video cassette tape, a compact disc, a cassette tape and a record token as presents for his brothers' birthdays, all of which are next week. Given the following information, what will each brother get?

Alan will not get the compact disc unless Barry gets the video cassette tape and David gets the cassette tape. Barry will not get the cassette tape unless Carl gets the record token and Alan gets the video cassette tape. David will not get the record token unless Alan gets the compact disc and Barry gets the video cassette tape. Alan will not get the video cassette tape unless Carl gets the record token and David gets the cassette tape. Barry will not get the video cassette tape unless Alan gets the record token and David gets the cassette tape. Alan will not get the record token unless Barry gets the compact disc and Carl gets the video cassette tape. Carl will not get the record token unless Barry gets the compact disc and Alan gets the cassette tape. Alan will not get the cassette tape unless Barry gets the record token and David gets the compact disc. Carl will not get the video cassette tape unless David gets the compact disc.

Q128 Combination* A88

The diagram below represents a dial on a safe which has 12 points, one of them black. The black point, presently pointing toward a black dot, is to be turned to each letter in turn, but not in alphabetical order, to open the safe. The dial should be turned toward the letters as follows.

A before D but after B. B before C but after H. H before F, F before G, G before I and I before J. H after K, K before F, F after D, D before G, and G after E. E before D, C before

E, E after B, C before G, and A after E.

What is the order of letters to which the black point should be turned in order to open the safe?

Q129　Odd One Out*****　A102

The diagrams below are that of a flattened cube and three views of the cube before it was flattened. Which of the three views is incorrect? (This time only two of the dotted lines along which the original cube was folded are shown.)

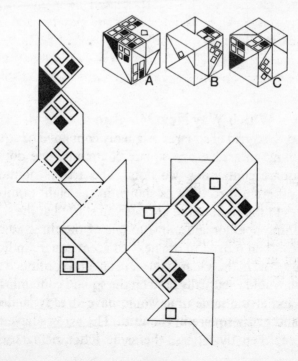

Q130 Logic Cube★★★★ A113

Fit the 26 letters of the alphabet and the symbol '@' into the cube of 27 smaller cubes. Each letter is to be fitted into one of the smaller cubes, as is the '@'. Remember that some of the smaller cubes are not visible in the diagram below.

H is below C which is below D. I is to the right of S, S is to the right of M, and M is below A, which in turn is to the left of J. X is below J and in front of V which is above Y. E is in front of Y and to the right of L. H is behind @ and I is in front of @. W is in front of G which is above V and to the right of Z. Z is behind U and above P. R is behind L. N is in front of O and above B. B is to the right of F which is in front of J. Q is to the right of K.

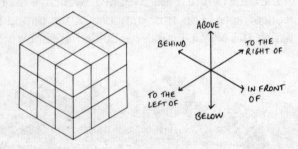

Q131 Which Way Next?★ A40

The 10 × 10 grid of squares originally contained 98 squares containing an arrow, one square containing one dot, and one square containing two dots. The arrows pointed in eight different directions as shown in the eight numbered squares to the right of the grid. If you started at the square containing one dot and move to one of the three adjacent squares, then moved to the next adjacent square indicated by the arrow in the square you were on, and continued to do so, you would eventually land on the square containing two dots; and at the same time would have already landed on each and every square in the grid. The arrows have since been replaced by letters, the same letter being used to replace the same type of arrow throughout the grid. See if you can work out which letter replaced each of the eight types of arrow.

A	A	A	D	B	E	E	A	A	••
C	B	E	E	F	H	D	A	G	B
F	G	F	E	H	H	F	D	G	C
F	C	D	C	H	H	B	F	A	C
D	C	H	H	D	B	G	F	A	G
H	A	F	G	C	D	D	G	F	G
C	E	D	C	D	B	C	H	B	C
H	B	H	H	D	C	D	B	A	C
C	H	G	B	E	H	B	B	F	G
•	H	E	H	E	E	A	H	A	C

1. ↑
2. ↗
3. →
4. ↘
5. ↓
6. ↙
7. ←
8. ↖

Q132 Blocked**** A133

Each of the 25 blocks shown below has been rotated about its centre, either 90° clockwise or 90° anticlockwise. When all of the 25 blocks are in their correct positions, all ten rows and columns contain the letters A to J only once. In which direction has each of the 25 blocks been rotated?

	A	B	C	D	E
1	E D / I J	D E / A B	F A / B G	C H / H J	C F / G I
2	G C / O E	I J / J H	D F / G C	E A / B F	I B / A H
3	F G / J H	F B / D E	H I / I J	C D / A G	C B / A E
4	B C / I B	A C / H F	A J / D E	F G / I E	J D / H G
5	A F / H A	G C / I G	C E / H B	D J / B I	E F / J D

91

Q133   Letter Boxes***   A9

When the diagram below is complete, each column and row should contain the letters A, B, C, D, E, F, G, H, I and J. See if you can complete the diagram by fitting the eight blocks of nine squares into the eight highlighted squares in the diagram, and then filling in the remaining squares in the diagram and the eight blocks.

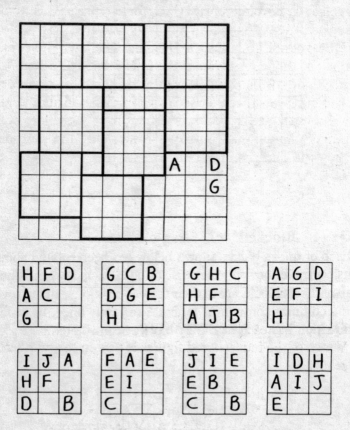

Q134 Clockwork Links**** A59

Diagram One is that of the numbers 1, 2, 3 and 4, each of which is surrounded by eight squares, all of which contain a different letter. The eight letters in the squares around each number can be rotated around the number either 90° clockwise, 90° anticlockwise or 180°. For example, if the letters around the number 1 were rotated 90° clockwise, A would replace C, B would replace G, C would replace K, G would replace J, etc.

Diagram Two is that of Diagram One after eight rotations of the letters around the four numbers – three 90° clockwise, two 90° anticlockwise and three through 180°. The letters have been rotated twice around each number. In what order, and in which direction, have the letters been rotated around each number to arrive at the positions shown in Diagram Two?

Diagram One

A	B	C	D	E
F	**1**	G	**2**	H
I	J	K	L	M
N	**3**	O	**4**	P
Q	R	S	T	U

Diagram Two

A	R	G	Q	E
K	**1**	J	**2**	N
C	L	O	T	H
O	**3**	U	**4**	P
B	M	I	S	F

Q135 What Next?*** A29

Which of the four lettered figures is next in the numbered sequence?

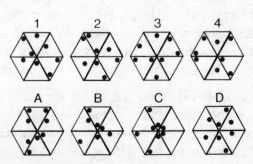

Q136 Logic Cube**** A103

Fit the 26 letters of the alphabet and the symbol '@' into the cube of 27 smaller cubes. Each letter is to be fitted into one of the smaller cubes, as is the '@'. Remember that some of the smaller cubes are not visible in the diagram below.

V is above H which is in front of S which is above E which is behind F which is to the right of M which is in front of X. A is above G which is above O which is behind I which is behind L which is to the right of Z which is to the right of R which is below J which is to the left of V. P is behind C which is to the left of U which is below N which is in front of D. K is above @, behind Q and to the left of Y which is above S. B is to the left of W and T is in front of Y.

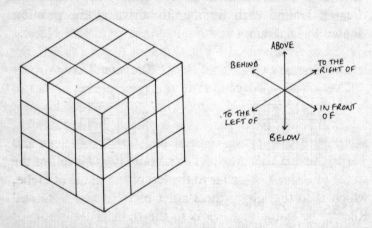

Q137 Temple Teaser***** A114

Recent excavations at a temple in Greece unearthed a wall in which there were a line of recesses. In each recess was a statue of a Greek goddess. Given the following jumbled-up information, list the names of the statues from right to left.

The statue of Iris is to the left of the statues of Nemesis, Pleiades, Hebe, Rhea, Nike, Ate and Moirai. The statue of Moirai is to the right of the statues of Ate and Hebe. The statue of Hebe is to the left of the statue of Ate which in turn is to the right of the statue of Amphitrite. The statue of Amphitrite is to the left of the statues of Iris, Terpsichore, Hebe and Hygiea. The statue of Hygiea is to the left of the statue of Chloris which is to the left of the statue of Iris which is to the right of the statue of Artemis which is to the left of the statues of Hebe, Amphitrite, Chloris and Pleiades.

The statues of Pleiades, Hestia, Hygiea, Selene, Eos and Artemis are all to the right of the statue of Hera which in turn is to the right of the statues of Aphrodite, Athene, Demeter, Hecate and Irene. The statue of Irene is to the left of the statues of Artemis and Persephone. The statue of Persephone is to the left of the statues of Amphitrite, Ate, Athene, Danae, Iris, Terpsichore, Tyche and Opis, and to the right of the statues of Aphrodite and Demeter. The statue of Demeter is to the left of the statues of Hecate, Hebe and Aphrodite, but the statue of Aphrodite is to the left of the statues of Irene, Eos, Chloris and Artemis.

The statue of Artemis is to the right of the statues of Athene and Eos, Eos's statue being to the left of Hygiea, which, in turn, is to the right of the statue of Opis, which, again in turn, is to the right of the statues of Selene and Terpsichore. The statue of Terpsichore is to the left of the statue of Chloris, which is to the left of the statue of Hebe, which is to the left of the statues of Nemesis, Nike and Rhea. The statue of Rhea is to the right of the statue of Nemesis and to the left of the statues of Ate and Nike. The statue of Nike is to the left of the statue of Ate. The statue of Danae is to the right of the statues of Athene, Hestia and Selene.

The statue of Selene is to the left of the statues of Hestia, Amphitrite and Hebe. The statue of Hebe is to the right of the statue of Pleiades, the statue of Hecate is to the left of the statues of Irene and Aphrodite, and the statue of Eos is to the right of the statue of Tyche. Finally, the statue of Tyche is to the right of the statues of Danae and Hestia.

The diagram below represents an aerial view of a room which has been divided into 100 squares, as shown by the dotted lines. In each of the squares there should be a dot marked on the floor in the centre of the square, or a double-sided mirror. When all of the dots and mirrors are in their correct places, a laser beam can enter the room at square A1 in the direction indicated by an arrow, and leave the room from square J10. At the same time, the laser beam shines over each and every dot marked on the floor. When the beam reaches a mirror it 'bounces off' at an angle of 90°, but it never crosses itself. If the beam hits the outside wall it is absorbed by the wall and can go no further.

Twenty of the dots/mirrors are not in place; eight dots (X), seven mirrors from lower left to upper right (Y), and five mirrors from upper left to lower right (Z). See if you can determine which of the squares containing '?' should be replaced by:

1. X squares;   2. Y squares;   3. Z squares.

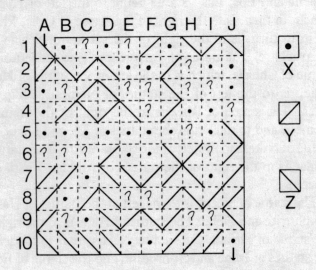

A does not live at numbers 1 or 17. F lives directly opposite B, K lives directly opposite N, and M lives directly opposite H. E does not live at numbers 5 or 7 but does live directly opposite P. C, N and G live in the same block of three houses as do B, J and P. The block in which B, J and P live is not the first block of houses you pass by if you walk clockwise past the houses. O lives directly opposite J, D lives directly opposite G, and Q lives directly opposite C. K, J and O each live in one of the houses which are in the centre of a block of three. L does not live in a block of three houses. P does not live at numbers 8 or 9, C does not live at 12 or 13, and I does not live at 9, 16 or 17. M lives in a house which is part of a block of three. If walking past the houses clockwise, the path to D's house is the path after the path to L's house, and you would arrive at B's house before J's.

Who lives in each of the 17 houses?

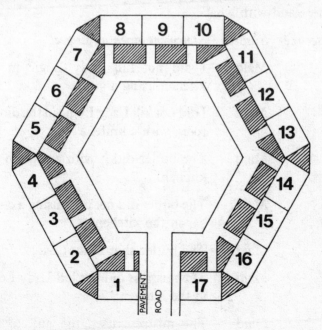

Q140   Whodunnit?★★★★★   A123

Just after the detectives working on the case of 'Who killed Lord Logic?' had completed their statements, all of the lights went out and there was a very loud scream. Two minutes later, the lights went back on again and Lady Logic was found lying dead in the hallway. There was quite a lot of blood on the floor and it looked as if her body had been dragged from either the kitchen or the dining room. The detective in charge called upon another two detectives who had just arrived at Logic Manor to help in solving this latest possible murder. A gun, a knife, a rope and a crowbar were found lying in the corner of the hallway. There were three people who could have murdered Lady Logic, all of whom were each interviewed by all seven detectives. Given the three people who could have murdered Lady Logic, a list of all 21 statements given to the seven detectives, and the fact that only seven of the 21 statements are true, who did it, where and with what?

Detective	Suspect	Statement given by suspect
1	Maid	I did not kill Lady Logic in the kitchen using a gun.
2	Maid	I did not kill Lady Logic in the dining room with a knife.
3	Maid	The butler did it with a rope in the kitchen.
4	Maid	The butler did not do it using a crowbar in the kitchen.
5	Maid	The butler shot Lady Logic.
6	Maid	The mistress did not kill Lady Logic in the kitchen.
7	Maid	The mistress used the gun to kill Lady Logic.

1	Butler	I murdered Lady Logic by stabbing her with a knife.
2	Butler	The maid used a gun to murder Lady Logic.
3	Butler	The mistress used a crowbar to kill Lady Logic.
4	Butler	The maid did not kill Lady Logic in the dining room.
5	Butler	The mistress used a rope to kill Lady Logic in the kitchen.
6	Butler	The maid used a knife to stab Lady Logic to death in the dining room.
7	Butler	The maid used a rope to hang Lady Logic in the dining room.
1	Mistress	The maid shot Lady Logic in the dining room.
2	Mistress	The butler hit Lady Logic over the head with a crowbar.
3	Mistress	The butler stabbed Lady Logic with a knife in the kitchen.
4	Mistress	The maid killed Lady Logic in the dining room with a crowbar.
5	Mistress	The maid killed Lady Logic using a knife in the dining room.
6	Mistress	I killed Lady Logic in the kitchen using a rope.
7	Mistress	I killed Lady Logic in the kitchen using a knife.

Q141 Odd One Out ★★★★★ A60

The diagrams below are that of a flattened cube and three
views of the cube before it was flattened. Which of the three
views is incorrect? (This time only two of the dotted lines
along which the original cube was folded are shown.)

Q142 3D Movement ★★★★★ A19

The diagram below is that of a large cube divided into 27
smaller cubes. I know that, if I start in the centre of the
smaller cube indicated by the arrow and move in the following directions in the following order, I will finish in the
centre of one of the four lettered cubes: right, down, left,
down, forward, up, right, backwards, left, down, right, up,
forward, down, backwards, left, forward and up. But I
don't know if I have to move a distance of one or two cubes
each time. One thing I do know is that I must pass through

100

the centre of all 27 cubes only once. See if you can work out the distance I must move in each of the 19 directions.

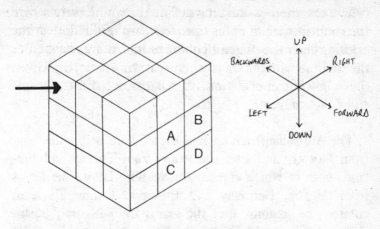

Q143   Grid Fill – Numbers****   A68
Fit the 36 numbers into the grid below.

07492	14679	14793	14987	18671	18962
23149	24693	26794	29183	35444	36794
41397	46578	49234	51709	56676	61341
63927	64139	64328	65896	67532	71934
73421	74321	75269	78261	78549	81432
84652	85679	89765	98532	98653	99289

Although there are never any winners or losers at the Logicalympics, there is one time during the whole event where the countries are in order one after another. This is at the opening ceremony when all of the participating teams enter the stadium with the team captain carrying their flag. Given the following information, in what order did the teams enter the stadium?

The Australian team entered the stadium before the team from Norway and after the teams from Turkey and Finland, both of which entered the stadium before the teams from Algeria, Germany and Ethiopia. Denmark's team entered the stadium after the teams from Algeria, Japan, Portugal, China and Venezuela. The team from Venezuela entered the stadium before the team from China and after the teams from Portugal and Japan. Both of the teams from Portugal and Japan entered the stadium before the teams from the USA, Sweden and China.

The team from Turkey entered the stadium before the team from Portugal, and the team from Greece entered the stadium before the team from Japan, but the teams from Algeria and Canada entered the stadium before both Portugal's team and the team from Japan. Japan's team entered the stadium after the teams from France, Hungary, Portugal and Finland. The team from Romania entered the stadium before the teams from Mexico, Norway, Greece, Finland, India and Canada, and the team from Canada entered the stadium before the teams from Algeria, France and Greece, but after the teams from Brazil, Great Britain, India and Spain. The team from Spain entered the stadium before the teams from Turkey and Romania both of which entered the stadium after the teams from Brazil and Hungary.

The team from Hungary entered the stadium before the teams from Austria and Brazil, the latter of which entered the stadium after the team from Austria but before the teams from Spain, India and France. The team from France entered the stadium before the team from Portugal who in turn entered before the team from Greece. The team from Germany entered the stadium after the teams from Great Britain and Mexico, but before the team from Ethiopia. The team from Mexico also entered the stadium before the team from Ethiopia.

The team from Algeria entered the stadium before the teams from New Zealand and Norway, as did the team from India. The teams from Denmark, Great Britain and New Zealand entered the stadium after the team from Turkey. The team from France entered the stadium after the teams from Norway and New Zealand and the team from New Zealand entered the stadium before the team from Australia. The team from Romania entered the stadium after the teams from Great Britain and Austria, the latter of which entered the stadium before the team from Spain. The team from Sweden entered the stadium before the team from Venezuela which in turn entered the stadium before the team from China. The team from Mexico entered the stadium after the team from Finland, and the team from Ethiopia entered the stadium before the team from India. The team from the USA entered after the team from Denmark.

When the grid below is complete, it contains the numbers 1 to 20 inclusive, 20 times each. Given that no column or row contains the same number more than once, see if you can fill in the missing numbers.

1	2	3	4	5	6	7	8	9	10	11	12	13	14	15	16	17	18	19	20
2	18	1		3			14		12				19					4	
3			16		15	1				6	17	5	8		2	14			
4			11			7	8			16		1	2	18		20			
5	15		11			9	2			16	4			14	13		8		
6		5				3	19	16	13	15		12		20					
7	10			1	15				14		12	17	4	5	9	16			
8		17	5	9		2		16	19	7			18	4		15	10	6	
9	11	10	19		15	14	16	17		2	4	5		6				13	
10		20		12	19	16	6		18	9		15		17	1	2		11	
11			10	6	17	13	7	3			2	14	8			16	4		9
12	5	11	20	17			13		2	16	1			7		15	10	6	
13	17	14	9		2				20		12		11	5		3			
14	13	16	15	10	9			5	8	7							20		18	19
15						9	10				3	4	14	13	19	20	17	18	
16		15		2			6	18	5		20	10	11	12	13	1	8		
17	12	9	3		5		18		4	1	19		13			11	7		
18			2		8	10	19		1	15	20		3	13			16	4	
19	9	7		1	11	5	20	8			17		16	2	12				
20	7		16		10	11	17		5	15	14			2	3		8	12	

One afternoon, in the A Class of the Academy for Advanced Academics, the 25 students were given a seating plan for the next lecture, but there were no names allocated to the seats. Instead, there was a set of clues with the plan. Given the same seating plan and set of clues as the Advanced Academics, see if you can determine where each of the 25 students should sit during the next lecture.

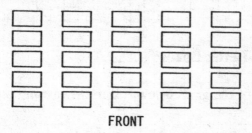

FRONT

Archy should sit behind Alred. Alroy should sit next to Askew. André, Aurel and Alred should sit in the same row. Alves should sit on Abram's right. Alwyn should sit in one of the four corner seats. Allan and Aaron should sit in the same row. Anson should sit on Abner's right. André should sit in front of Alwin and Aubyn. Alban should sit on Abram's left. Aaron should sit in front of Ariel, Alves and Abner. Alban should sit in front of Alwyn. Airay should sit behind Angus and Alroy. Abdul should sit behind Aubyn. Algie should not sit in the front row. Anson should sit in the same row as Alwin. Athol should sit in front of Anson. André should sit in one of the four corners. Alban should sit in front of Anton. Aaron should sit behind Askew. Aubyn should sit on Airay's right. Allan should sit between Aaron and Archy. Algie should not sit in the back row. Amand should not sit in the same row as Allan. Albat should sit in front of Anton.

('Sit behind' or 'sit in front of' means in the same column, but not necessarily next to each other. All of the students should sit facing the front of the class.)

Q147 Cubes★ A176

Which two cubes from 1 to 6 cannot be made from the flattened cube?

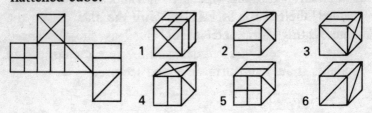

Q148 Letter Boxes★ A202

In each of the grids below, fill in the missing boxes.

1

J	A	J	?
F	M	A	?
M	J	S	?

2

A	C	L	?
A	G	P	?
C	L	S	?

Q149 Numbers★★ A148

What is the next number in each of these sequences?
★   A) 15, 20, 20, 6, 6, 19, 19, 5, 14, 20, 5, ?
★   B) 1, 8, 11, 18, 80, ?
★   C) 1, 2, 4, 14, 21, 22, 24, 31, ?
★★ D) 4, 1, 3, 1, 2, 4, 3, ?
★★ E) 1, 2, 4, 7, 28, 33, 198, ?
★★ F) 17, 8, 16, 23, 28, 38, 49, 62, ?
★★ G) 27, 216, 279, 300, ?
★★ H) 9, 7, 17, 79, 545, ?
★★ I) 2, 3, 10, 12, 13, 20, ?
★★ J) 34, 58, 56, 60, 42, ?

Q150 Words** A214

1 COMPATIBLE is to CURIE as AUDIENCE is to which of the following:
FREQUENT OCEANIC ROADSIDE
UNDERGONE UNSEEN

2 SOUND = 188
   HELD = 70
   OFTEN = 177
   CRAZY = 271
   ANSWER = ?

Q151 Age Old Question** A195

Dave is younger than Fred and older than George.
Alan is younger than Ian and older than Colin.
Ian is younger than George and older than John.
John is younger than Colin and older than Edward.
Fred is younger than Barry and older than Harry.
Harry is older than Dave.
WHO IS THE YOUNGEST?

Q152 Missing Letters** A165

What are the two missing letters?
? K O ? I N E F A

Q153 Logic Path** A230

Starting at the letter L and working across the grid to the letter H, see how many different ways you can find of collecting the letters LOGICPATH in the correct order. You may move in any direction, one square at a time, and may only collect nine letters each time.

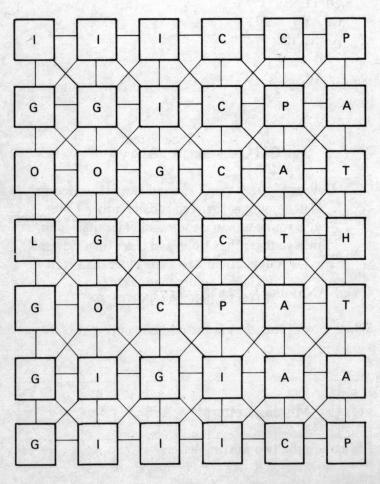

Q154   What Next?**   A157

What is the next letter in the following sequence?
U, A, R, H, E, U, ?

Q155   Letter Sequence**   A238

What is the next letter in the following sequence?
O E T E F E S N N E E ?

Q156   Sequence**   A147

Where should the number 10 be placed to continue the sequence?
8   5   4   9   1   7   6   3   2

Q157   Two Halves**   A186

If the letters from A to M = 202, what do the letters from N to Z = ?

Q158   Number Boxes**   A171

Which box of numbers is the odd one out?

A

5	8	3
1	4	6
7	2	9

B

6	5	8
3	1	4
9	7	2

C

4	8	2
1	5	7
6	3	9

What is the next letter in this sequence?

A B H F M C I G T D O J U ?

Divide the grid below into four equal parts, each of which should be the same shape and contain 16 letters. The 16 letters should then be arranged to form a 16-letter word. Each of the four parts contains a different word.

L	I	B	N	C	I	S	C
H	I	I	I	E	O	R	I
E	I	I	M	S	M	E	I
R	R	E	S	P	P	N	N
N	U	P	M	A	R	U	T
S	E	O	N	T	D	O	A
B	S	S	I	N	N	O	D
L	Y	T	R	G	I	N	N

Q161 One-word** A205

All of the following are one-word anagrams:

1 Avertible	7 Immersing	13 Anacruses
2 Coastline	8 Adulation	14 Arsenical
3 Decimated	9 Antidotes	15 Continuer
4 Relatives	10 Argentine	16 Lancaster
5 Optically	11 Mobilises	17 Pignorate
6 Introduce	12 Gyrations	18 Analogist

Q162 One-word** A150

All of the following are one-word anagrams:

1 Acetamide	7 Acierated	13 Adminicle
2 Cretinoid	8 Grandiose	14 Catechism
3 Largition	9 Canoeists	15 Gradients
4 Esperanto	10 Bacterial	16 Alignment
5 Runcinate	11 Aniconism	17 Ceilinged
6 Savourily	12 Cognition	18 Inoculant

Q163 One-word** A216

All the following are one-word anagrams:

1 Excitation	6 Nutriments
2 Shattering	7 Alphametic
3 Neologisms	8 Indicatory
4 Catalogued	9 Percussion
5 Gingersnap	10 Alarmingly

Q164 One-word** A178

All of the following are one-word anagrams:

1 Enumeration	8 Permeations
2 Adulterines	9 Desecration
3 Catapultier	10 Procreation
4 Inbreathing	11 Consumerist
5 Memorialist	12 Credentials
6 Enterprises	13 Conservation
7 Colonialist	14 Delicateness

Q165 Anagrams*** A241

All of the following are one-word anagrams. There are no links of meaning between the ten words and the groups.

1 Am a tall gray manic.
2 I, if Ada quit Colin's.
3 Present it to Martin.
4 Boy, I split rein sir.
5 Past idiot in tiger.
6 A green chain belt.
7 Leper's neat ration.
8 And suns grind time.
9 Mistrust ant Neil
10 The Martian island is in a bit mess.

Q166 Two in One*** A225

Each of the following groups of words contain two separate one-word anagrams of half the words in the group.
1 Stan dine built crest tuned meter.
2 I noticed boy spilt in faint I rise.
3 If I'm in a sly aged van, clip out oats.
4 I chart ice cap I print sheep carts.
5 Lift a coin call a timid ploy Issac.

Q167 Triplegram★★★★ A161

B and C are anagrams of A. A is a ten-letter word, each letter of which has been replaced by a number. No letter occurs more than once in each word. A, B and C are in alphabetical order.

A	1	2	3	4	5	6	7	8	9	10
B	1	3	2	4	5	6	7	8	9	10
C	4	5	1	2	3	6	7	8	9	10

Q168 Anagram Blocks★★★★ A253

In each of the following there are six blocks of three letters. Unscramble all 18 letters to form a word, using all of the letters only once. No two adjoining letters of the word formed should appear in the same block, *e.g.* the letter 'Y' in word A would not adjoin the letters 'P' or 'E'.

A

I P A	P Y E
O O T	D S R
R I N	O T L

B

O P E	S C B
S H L	I N N
E E E	S R M

C

E T B	A M A
T I I	N N R
L H E	S A S

D

C C Y	A A A
H T R	C E S
I L I	T L R

Q169   Triplegram****   A199

B and C are anagrams of A. A is a ten-letter word, each letter of which has been replaced by a number. No letter occurs more than once in each word. A, B and C are in alphabetical order.

A	1	2	3	4	5	6	7	8	9	10
B	2	7	8	10	5	1	6	4	9	3
C	10	9	1	6	4	8	2	5	7	3

Q170   Logic Box*   A175

Using the following clues, place the letters A to I inclusive into the grid. A is above D and in the same row as I. B is above F, above I, and to the right of G. C is above H and below G. D is between F and H in the same row. ('Above/below' refers to two letters in the same column. 'Left of/right of' refers to two letters in the same row.)

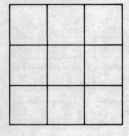

Q171 Logic Box** A231

Place the letters A, B, C, D, E, F, G, H and I into the grid of 9 squares using the following information:

I is in the same column as E which is not in the centre column. D is in the row below the row which contains F. A is in the row below the row which contains B. B is not in the first column. E is in the same row as F. C is in one of the four corner squares. G is in the square above A. F is in the same row as A, and in the same column as C. E is in the row below the row which contains B. H is in the same row as I, the same column as F, and is in a corner square.

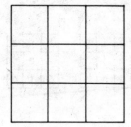

Q172 Smile Please** A169

In a recent competition all 11 contestants lined up in a straight line to have their photograph taken for the local newspaper. So that the winner would stand out from the other contestants, the winner was asked to stand on a box in the centre of the line-up. Alec and Alma stood to the right of the box, Adam stood to the right of Alroy, two people stood between Aaron and Aubyn, Archy and Adrian stood to the left of the box, six people stood between Alma and Aaron, seven people stood between Alston and Albert, Antony and Adrian stood either side of Aaron and two people stood between Aaron and Archy. Who won the competition?

Q173 One Missing** A245

Fit the nine small squares into the diagram to form a large square, each row and column of which should contain the letters A, B, C, D, E, F, G, H, I and J. What are the nine missing letters, and in which order should they be placed into grid E?

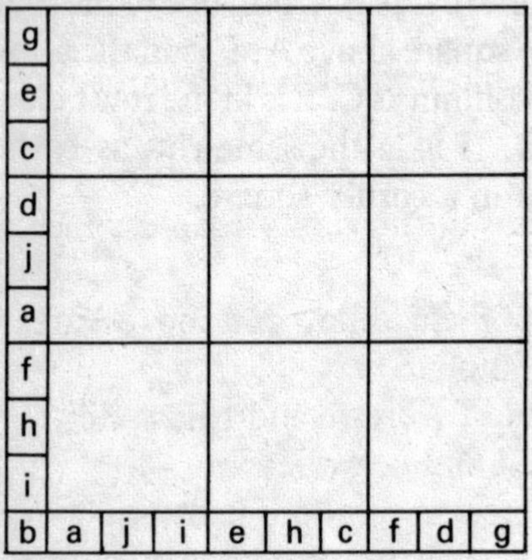
g
e
c
d
j
a
f
h
i
b a j i e h c f d g

A

j	g	e
f	d	c
b	e	j

B

j	h	e
d	g	h
i	j	b

C

e	f	g
h	i	d
d	h	b

D

h	b	a
a	e	j
g	f	d

E

F

h	j	a
g	b	e
j	g	f

G

a	d	b
i	f	j
f	e	d

H

b	c	i
c	a	f
e	i	c

I

d	c	i
b	i	g
c	a	h

There are 16 shelves on a wall which are arranged as shown in the diagram below. On each shelf there is a tin of paint, each containing a different type of Yellow. Using the following information, see if you can determine which type of yellow paint is on each of the 16 shelves.

Amber is below Fallow which is to left of Cream and Topaz.

Sulphur is below Buff and to the left of Primrose.

Cream is below Xanthic which is also to the left of Primrose.

Lemon and Guilded are to the right of Gold which is below Topaz.

Gamboge is to the left of Plain Yellow and above Aureate which is to the right of Sulphur.

Primrose is to the right of Aureate and below Gilt.

Saffron is above Lemon and below Gilt.

To the left or right of refers to paint tins in the same row. Above or below refers to paint tins in the same column.

1	2	3	4
5	6	7	8
9	10	11	12
13	14	15	16

Before King Arthur's knights sat down at the round table, they used to hang their shields on a rack as shown in the diagram below. Each shield was either red, white or blue, and was decorated with a circle or square, these again in either red, white or blue. Both rows of shields contained two shields and shapes of all three colours. No shield was the same colour as the shape painted on the shield itself. No red shield was next to, or above another red shield, but a red shape was above another red shape. Number one shield belonged to Bedivere and was white with a blue square. Number six shield belonged to Gawain and was blue with a red square. Number nine shield belonged to Tristram and was blue with a white circle. Launfal had a red shield with a blue circle, which was next to Mordred's white shield with a red circle. Calidore had a red shield with a white circle. Bors and Lancelot had red shields, Galahad and Percivale had white shields, and Pelleas and Geraint had blue shields. Percivale's shield was next to Calidore's and above Tristram's. The shield above Lancelot's had a circle the same colour as the shape on Galahad's shield. No blue shield was above another blue shield. To which knight did shield number 12 belong?

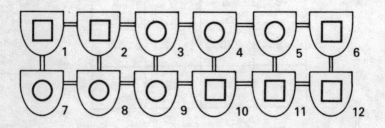

Diagram A contains the first 23 letters of the alphabet and the numbers one to four. Imagine that the eight letters surrounding each number can rotate around that number clockwise or anticlockwise. To arrive at diagram B, each of the numbers has been rotated twice, except number one, which has only been rotated once. See if you can work out the order in which they were rotated to arrive at diagram B, and, if they were rotated 90° or 180°, clockwise or anticlockwise.

A

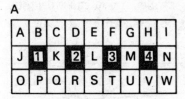

B

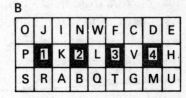

The diagram below is a view looking down on a room 10ft square. The room has been divided into 100 smaller squares, as shown by the dotted lines. In each square there is a dot marked on the floor, or a double-sided mirror. When all the dots and mirrors are in place, a laser beam enters the room at A1 and leaves the room at J10, at the same time covering all of the dots in the room. When the beam reaches a mirror, it bounces off at an angle of 45°, as shown in square A3. Ten of the dots/mirrors are not in place; four dots (x), four mirrors from right to left (y), and two mirrors from left to right (z). See if you can work out what each of the 10 ?s should be replaced by: x, y or z.

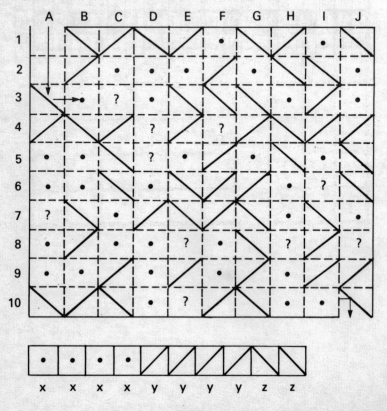

120

Complete the grid so that each row and column contains the letters

T H I N K P O W E R

				T					R
	R					T	E		
R		T				W			
			T		O		R		
			P			R	T		
	T		K		R				
		N		R					T
	I		R		T				
	H	T	R						
T		R							

Q179   Block Total*   A182

Each of the five letters in the word block has a different value between one and ten. Using the totals next to the grid, work out the value of each letter.

B	L	O	C	K	33
B	O	K	B	B	33
L	O	K	K	K	24
L	C	C	K	O	34
O	C	L	B	B	37

35   35   29   33   29

Q180 A Good Year* A168

Thirteen different years are listed next to the grid below. Using the digit totals next to each column and row, fit the 13 years into the grid, vertically or horizontally. Some of the years overlap, and each column and row contains at least one year. Two digits and one year have been entered for you as a start.

	6	19	16	21	20	20		
1121						9	27	1433
1189						1	17	1452
1194		4				4	19	1468
1232						3	26	1711
1272						3	13	1873
1426								1921
								1941

1433
1452
1468
1711
1873
1921
1941

123

Each letter of the alphabet has been given a different value from 1 to 26. Next to the list of words are the total values of the letters contained in each word. What is the value of each letter of the alphabet?

BEG = 59   CALL = 48   CHIEF = 36
CRAZY = 60   DEN = 53

GAME = 47   GUN = 51   HAM = 16
HAVE = 40   IF = 11

JACK = 24   KEY = 43   LAZE = 57
MAP = 28   MOVE = 58

NEON = 86   OXEN = 82   PALM = 47   QUIT = 40

QUITE = 60   STALL = 80   TALK = 39
TORE = 73   VAST = 51   WALK = 54

The diagram below represents the layout of a new prison. There are 21 guards, 45 prisoners, six towers for the guards and five compounds for the prisoners. The towers are numbered 1 to 6 and the compounds lettered A to E. All of the compounds are triangular in shape and have a guard tower at each of the three corners. The number of prisoners in a compound is equal to the total number of guards in the towers on the corners of the compound. Given that there are 11 prisoners in compound A, one guard in tower number two, four guards in tower number three, and no two towers or compounds contain the same number of guards or prisoners, how many guards are there in each of the six towers?

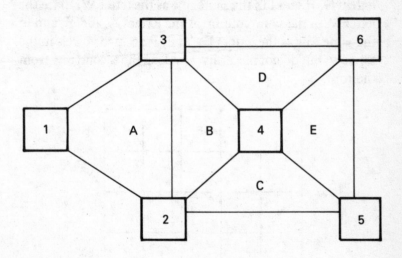

Number the letters of the alphabet A–Z, 1 to 26 respectively, then delete the letter 'X'. Using the information given, place the remaining 25 letters into the diagram. Three letters are already in place.

The totals next to the columns, rows and diagonal lines, are the total value of the letters to be placed in the column, row or diagonal line. The value of the letters U and F are 21 and 6, therefore the value of the remaining letters in the centre column is 22. The letter S should be placed in a square diagonally adjacent to the square containing the letter O. The centre column should contain three vowels. Place the letters Z, H and T in the same column. Place the letters G, H and I in the same row as the letter W. Place the letter M in the same column as the letters W and Y, and in the same row as the letters E and F. Place two vowels in the top row, but do not place any vowels in the second row from the top.

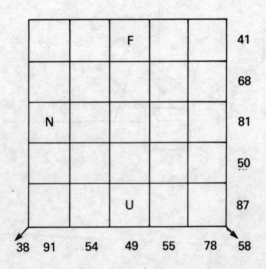

126

The whole numbers from 1 to 15 inclusive have been re-placed by letters in the diagram below. Given that A+D+G+J+M=B+E+H+K+N=C+F+I+L+O, the three letters in each pentagon total three-fifths of A+D+G+J+M, J = 1/3 C, E = 1/3 K, I = 1/3 N and B = 1/3 J: what is the value of each letter in the diagram?

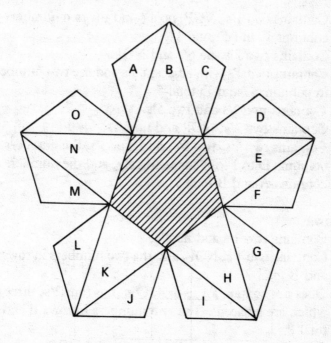

Q185 Numerical Logic*** A239

The diagram opposite should contain the numbers one to six, six times each; the numbers next to the grid itself are the row and column number totals. Using the following 12 clues complete the diagram. (NOP means no other pairs of numbers.)

Across

A Contains two 1's, NOP, no 4's and the two numbers in columns E and F total 11.

B Contains two 2's, no 6's and NOP.

C Contains two 4's, two adjacent 3's and the two numbers in columns C and D total 5.

D Contains two 1's and two 5's.

E Contains two 3's, NOP and no 5's.

F Contains two 5's, two 6's, no 1's or 3's, the numbers in columns D to F run consecutively, and the numbers in columns A and B total 7.

Down

A Contains two 1's and no 4's.

B Contains two 4's, NOP, and the two numbers in rows A and B total 7.

C Does not contain a 1, 3 or 4. Contains four 2's, three of which are adjacent. The two numbers in rows E and F total 8.

D Contains two adjacent 1's, two 3's and NOP.

E Contains two 5's, NOP and no 4's.

F Contains three 4's but no 1's or 2's.

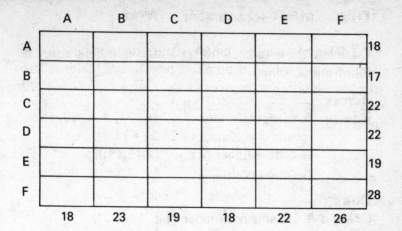

	A	B	C	D	E	F	
A							18
B							17
C							22
D							22
E							19
F							28
	18	23	19	18	22	26	

Q186 Mini Crossnumber★ A158

Complete the diagram with six 3-digit numbers, using the following six clues:

Across

Row A   A triangular number +1 (*e.g.* 1, 3, 6, 10, 15 . . . formed by adding 1+2+3+4+5 . . .).

B   A cube number (*e.g.* 27 (3×3×3)).

C   A cube number.

Down

Column A   A square number (*e.g.* 4 (2×2)).

B   A cube number.

C   A triangular number.

	A	B	C
A	1		
B			
C			

Q187 Jigsum★★ A180

Fit the twenty pieces into the diagram opposite. When complete, all 14 calculations should equal the totals given next to the diagram. Each calculation is to be treated sequentially and should start at a square indicated by an arrow, then follow the direction of the arrow to the answer on the other side of the grid.

There are six horizontal, six vertical, and two diagonal calculations.

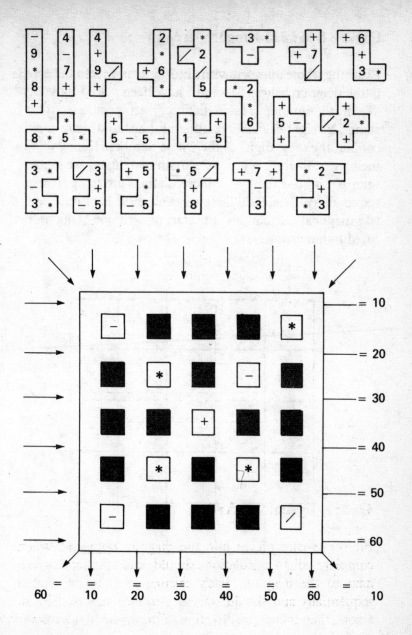

131

Q188 0 to 12 in Nine** A193

Place the whole numbers from 1 to 9 inclusive into the gaps in the diagram below (3, 4 and 5 have been placed for you.) When all numbers are in their correct positions, there should be eight calculations, the solutions to which should contain the same digits as the whole numbers from 0 to 12 inclusive. All eight solutions contain two digits, are higher than 10 and less than 90. All calculations are to be treated sequentially. There are three vertical, three horizontal and two diagonal calculations, the start of each one being indicated by an arrow.

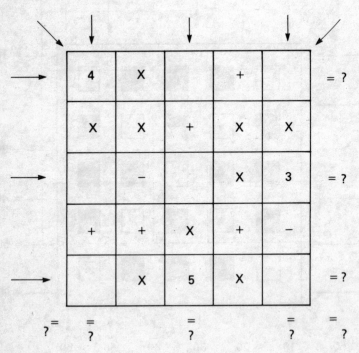

Add together five different numbers from the grid below to achieve the highest possible total. Starting at column A and working your way across to column E, you may only choose one number from each column, and no two numbers may be from the same row or diagonal line.

A	B	C	D	E
1	7	13	20	6
25	9	2	23	11
14	22	17	8	16
4	12	10	3	19
24	18	5	15	21

The answer to each of the clues is a 3-digit prime number.
The clue for each number is the total of the digits multiplied
together.

Across		Down	
A	12	**A**	36
D	63	**B**	189
E	36	**C**	21
G	189	**E**	36
H	98	**F**	270
K	10	**G**	3
L	252	**H**	84
M	81	**I**	14
N	27	**J**	441
P	21	**N**	8
Q	48	**O**	162
R	63	**P**	63

Q191 Connection*** A234

What is the connection between 567 and 854?

Q192 Bullseye*** A166

Three darts players playing 501 up have had three turns (A, B and C), each with three darts each turn. From the information given below, which player can finish with a bull (50) on their 10th dart?

Player 1
A   An odd score more than 70.
B   Scored 180.
C   An even number, more than player 3's turn B + 1.

Player 2
A   One score less than player 1's turn B.
B   Two thirds of player 1's turn B.
C   An even score more than 160.

Player 3
A   17 more than turn C.
B   The lowest even score of all nine turns.
C   An odd score more than 100.

Numbers finish at the thicker lines, no two answers are the same and 17 digits have been entered as a guide.

Across
1 Square   4 Square   7 Cube   9 Prime   10 Prime
11 Cube   12 Square   14 Square   15 Square   16 Cube
19 Square   22 Square   24 Prime   25 Prime   26 Prime
27 Prime   28 Square   29 Square

Down
2 Square   3 Square   4 Prime   5 Square   6 Prime
7 Cube   8 Cube   10 Square   13 Cube   17 Prime
18 Square   19 Square   20 Prime   21 Square   23 Prime
25 Prime

1	2		3	4	5		6
1 5	**2**	8	**3**	**4** 6	**5**	**6** 6
7	2	**8**	**9**	5	**10** 3	
	11			**12**		**13** 1
14				**15** 8		
16	**17**	**18**		**19** 2	**20**	**21**
22		4	**23**	**24** 3		8
25 1		**26**		1	**27** 1	
28	9			**29**		

Q194   Number Sequence 1★★★★   A242

What is the missing number?

1980   2961   3870   ?   9108

Q195   Number Sequence 2★★★★   A224

What is the next number in this sequence?

1   6   18   40   35   66   112   176   117   190   286   408   ?

Q196   All in Line★   A198

Find a 3-letter word that can be prefixed by all of the following letters to form another word:

B   D   F   H   J   M   N   P   R   S   T   V   W

Q197   Ending★   A152

Find the word ending that can be prefixed by all of the following:

B   CL   D   H   J   L   M   PL   R   S   SL   T   TH

Q198   Which Word?★★   A162

Which word is the odd one out?

BYE   CAN   GEE   PAW   POT   TAM   TAR   TOM

Q199   Allsorts**   A249

Arrange the following into groups of four:

ALERTING   NITRATES
ARGENTIC   REACTING
CATERING   REAGENTS
CREATING   RELATING
ESTRANGE   SERGEANT
GREATENS   STRAITEN
INTEGRAL   TERTIANS
INTREATS   TRIANGLE

Q200   Prefix***   A226

In each of the following, find a word which can prefix all of the words in each group to form another word.

1 Rhyme, Stalk, Water.
2 Brush, Frame, Tight.
3 Plate, Straw, Table.
4 Bark, Dish, Less, Root, Wort.
5 Body, Day, Time, Ways, What.
6 Able, Book, Over, Port, Word.
7 Boy, Flower, Point, Room.
8 Bench, Let, On, Runner, Wise.
9 Land, Penny, Plate, Pole, Weed, Word.
10 Dog, Fish, Light, Sail, Shade.
11 Brain, Down, Jaw, Pot, Rope, Up.
12 Age, Ball, Berry, Bind, Bottle, Brash, Ice, Pipe.

Q201   Letter Blocks***   A218

Arrange the following 36 blocks, each containing two letters, to form 12 six-letter words. The initial letters of the 12 words are:

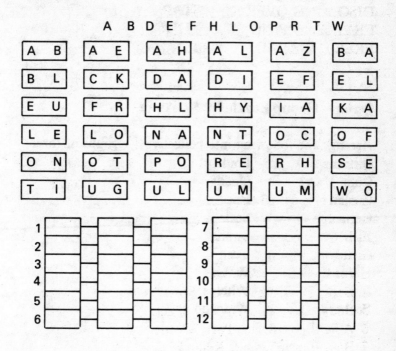

Q202   Mr Hoan***   A251

Mr Hoan has eight favourite letters, six of which are H, L, S, P, N and M. What are Mr Hoan's two other favourite letters?

Q203   Group Puzzle***   A244

Arrange the following words into groups of three:

ABLE	HERB	SELF
BACK	KING	SLAP
DISC	OVER	STAR
FEAT	PING	THIN
FREE	RAIN	TING

Q204   Group Puzzle****   A232

Arrange the following into collective(!) groups of three:

Bitterns	Poultry
Cubs	Quails
Curlews	Roes
Cranes	Seals
Fish	Swans
Goats	Teal
Herons	Whales
Pigs	Whelps
Pochards	Widgeon

Q205   What's in a Name****   A246

Arrange the following into three groups of three:

COLIN   FRANK   HAZEL   ELLEN   GLEN
BERYL   RALPH   RUBY   DOUGLAS

Q206   Qwerty*****   A154

What are the two longest words that can be typed using the top row of the typewriter keyboard?

This puzzle and the following ten are all letter grids where a number of words are hidden. Words may be found vertically, horizontally, diagonally, forwards or backwards, but always in a straight line. The letters left after all the words have been found will reveal the final word.

Find 31 capitals of various countries, and reveal another capital.

```
T  O  C  A  N  N  E  I  V  L  M  O  K  A
S  R  T  P  F  N  B  I  M  L  U  I  H  I
E  A  E  U  R  O  E  E  O  A  V  O  S  N
P  N  L  E  P  N  L  H  L  A  D  L  E  U
A  G  B  I  T  A  K  A  J  G  A  R  H  S
D  O  S  I  S  C  M  K  U  M  R  S  I  B
U  O  A  U  O  B  Y  S  A  K  I  A  U  D
B  N  R  T  C  E  U  B  T  D  U  J  D  A
E  E  S  A  R  S  A  R  A  E  U  N  W  E
J  H  I  A  A  D  A  G  Y  M  R  A  A  N
A  R  B  I  N  I  O  M  B  G  T  D  N  A
O  A  G  A  F  M  E  U  A  T  E  L  A  M
T  O  U  O  N  A  R  R  O  D  N  A  G  M
N  L  S  G  N  A  Y  G  N  O  Y  P  A  A
```

Q208 Letter Grid – Vehicles** A210

Find 28 types of vehicle, and reveal a vehicle name which is usually shortened.

```
A P Y N C R A C E L B B U B
K M A E E A O E W T U N A R
I V B D R A B A E L A N A B
O Q N U C R H L L D D E A R
R E U H L S U D E W L C S R
T M E A K A O S A C M B C T
E O S C D Z N G Y O A N O S
N U I N E R O C S N E R O D
N R A R L N I N E R I T T A
E L H A A R A G A T B A E O
D U C K T H O L A R U N R R
T E L O C A C D R O S K Y T
```

Q209 Letter Grid – Dogs** A236

Find 25 types/breed of dog, and reveal the last word of a quotation attributed to Aldous Huxley (1894–1963).
'To his dog, every man is . . . .'

```
D G U R D Y B R I G N B M C
R A C H K N E L O K E A Y A
C P L S O T U D E D U N L I
D H U M N E P O L N A L R R
E H I I A E N I H I H E A N
E S O H E T N A N Y Z E A S
R P E H U G I A D U E I I B
H A S N T A R A A T T R E M
O N T O I E H N N A A A G G
U I N T M K H U S L G E E U
N E O O E C E L A L C U R P
D L P N S R A P E L O H D G
```

Q210   Letter Grid – Hats**   A181

Find 26 types of hats, and reveal a line from a song connected with hats.

```
P  W  H  E  N  G  L  E  N  G  A  R  R  Y
A  R  A  E  O  I  V  T  I  L  E  R  E  D
N  R  V  I  S  B  K  E  P  I  E  Y  E  L
A  A  A  T  T  U  Y  N  M  L  B  E  Y  H
M  S  L  E  S  I  N  W  S  R  R  O  H  H
A  O  C  N  T  K  F  O  U  S  E  M  A  P
T  M  A  O  S  E  B  B  T  T  B  R  E  T
R  B  L  R  Z  T  D  A  U  E  A  E  S  S
I  R  A  O  H  E  L  O  R  F  K  R  H  A
L  E  B  C  R  K  B  G  T  E  T  A  E  P
B  R  T  B  E  S  M  I  D  I  K  Y  A  B
Y  O  Y  R  P  O  T  H  M  O  O  C  M  E
```

143

Q211   Letter Grid – Professions**   A184

Find 35 professions, occupations and trades, and reveal an
occupation which no longer exists.

```
R  R  L  P  R  B  R  R  R  E  R  A  N  R
A  C  E  U  E  A  E  E  E  S  A  M  R  E
S  V  H  I  R  P  I  L  M  T  M  R  D  L
R  S  O  A  L  M  P  R  L  E  N  I  U  T
U  E  E  C  U  E  A  E  R  E  T  I  I  N
B  H  X  T  A  F  T  I  T  O  R  L  A  P
S  O  S  E  T  L  F  O  R  E  E  I  P  P
R  O  S  S  D  L  I  E  H  R  E  I  N  B
C  E  M  U  O  N  L  S  U  S  A  R  E  A
P  A  K  R  N  L  I  G  T  R  T  L  E  R
N  L  I  A  E  L  M  A  I  S  L  R  N  E
I  S  V  M  B  A  I  S  I  B  I  G  V  K
T  V  A  U  K  N  T  T  O  U  B  P  O  N
Y  N  P  E  E  H  R  Y  Q  T  E  A  Y  I
E  R  R  R  N  A  M  S  D  N  U  O  R  T
```

Q212   Letter Grid – Dances***   A203

Find 24 dances, and reveal another dance.

```
T  P  Y  E  P  B  O  S  S  A  N  O  V  A
A  R  V  E  O  O  A  G  L  H  U  G  S  L
E  I  I  L  P  R  O  L  N  N  I  A  I  E
J  U  E  P  A  S  E  K  O  A  L  M  N  J
R  R  Q  B  U  T  H  T  A  T  D  I  M  E
O  V  A  S  N  D  S  T  A  P  R  N  P  Y
N  N  A  A  E  E  I  R  A  U  O  I  A  B
D  J  R  L  L  B  E  A  O  R  P  O  K  F
O  A  A  R  E  L  A  B  R  N  T  S  K  O
T  L  A  B  L  T  M  R  R  Y  T  S  N  A
E  H  O  O  U  A  A  O  A  O  B  M  A  M
C  P  S  K  T  J  H  E  N  I  U  G  E  B
```

Q213 Letter Grid – Groups*** A240

Find 29 group names, and reveal the group name for apes.

B	M	S	N	S	K	U	L	K	F	L	O	C	K
E	R	U	D	O	W	N	M	O	H	L	H	R	C
V	G	O	R	E	I	U	W	M	O	A	U	L	D
Y	N	G	O	M	R	T	R	R	T	H	O	S	P
E	I	N	R	D	U	A	A	T	E	W	C	A	H
L	R	I	E	E	H	R	E	T	D	T	D	S	K
G	E	R	M	C	D	R	A	E	L	D	S	I	C
G	H	P	T	R	I	N	R	T	L	A	N	U	U
A	T	S	A	N	A	N	U	I	I	D	X	E	M
G	A	I	G	C	I	W	N	O	L	O	P	E	S
C	G	W	N	D	K	G	S	E	S	E	N	E	S
S	N	I	E	K	S	B	U	I	L	D	I	N	G

Q214 Letter Grid – Rivers*** A173

Find 33 rivers from various countries, and reveal another river.

W	W	R	E	H	C	I	R	T	I	S	H	C
A	V	O	C	A	L	H	P	N	A	L	L	A
N	N	S	R	A	Y	U	I	P	I	A	O	W
G	I	E	Y	R	T	A	G	N	R	M	I	E
A	R	A	D	U	A	U	N	E	D	N	R	S
N	C	E	M	E	A	Y	N	E	N	W	E	E
U	K	A	T	D	L	C	U	I	T	D	I	R
I	Y	E	I	S	E	A	P	R	E	O	I	N
O	S	A	N	J	E	E	W	O	U	M	O	S
T	N	A	A	N	G	I	L	A	R	A	E	K
A	W	N	I	N	E	U	N	B	R	A	R	N
S	U	T	A	A	S	B	M	D	M	E	L	I
D	A	R	I	B	B	L	E	T	I	A	S	I
G	O	D	A	R	O	L	O	C	I	I	H	P

145

Q215 Letter Grid – Ports*** A247

Find 32 ports from around the world, and reveal a port in Egypt.

```
E  T  M  P  A  K  Y  F  I  O  S  A  K  A
L  A  U  O  I  D  L  O  A  A  D  L  T  E
L  L  N  V  U  U  A  Y  K  E  H  T  K  G
A  E  R  E  S  L  R  N  L  O  E  I  I  X
G  A  H  H  L  A  M  A  I  I  H  S  E  A
L  E  I  A  E  S  I  E  M  K  B  A  L  W
P  N  V  L  K  D  I  A  I  O  A  I  M  N
G  E  N  A  E  O  D  N  R  N  N  K  A  A
A  U  E  M  T  A  D  N  O  I  N  V  C  K
D  R  D  D  N  A  E  A  R  R  A  E  A  H
E  E  A  A  A  A  M  A  T  R  E  N  S  O
N  B  C  W  G  R  T  A  I  E  R  I  S  D
D  O  O  I  T  A  A  N  T  A  R  C  A  K
C  O  R  K  M  M  O  P  V  I  A  E  R  A
```

Q216 Letter Grid – Composers*** A196

Find 27 composers, and reveal another composer.

```
S  O  U  S  A  E  B  L  N  R  E  K  T
K  L  F  E  T  E  L  E  B  Y  R  D  C
O  R  N  F  L  R  V  R  K  Y  M  D  I
I  R  E  L  E  O  A  S  A  O  U  K  D
A  N  I  I  H  N  Z  N  E  S  C  D  E
S  N  I  T  S  I  B  T  O  N  S  O  N
I  U  E  T  V  L  E  A  E  M  O  U  E
C  E  I  A  N  V  E  R  C  A  R  P  B
B  W  R  L  E  O  A  R  E  H  G  E  B
I  T  E  R  E  Z  P  L  S  L  S  R  R
S  V  D  A  B  B  G  S  T  E  K  I  L
B  I  E  C  E  A  I  R  I  R  Y  N  I
X  A  B  S  R  Y  S  S  U  B  E  D  N
```

Find 29 words connected with heraldry, and reveal an
appropriate quotation attributed to Richard I (1157–1199)
in 1198.

```
F  D  D  R  A  D  N  A  T  S  D  I  S  E
R  H  L  Y  G  N  E  Z  O  L  U  E  T  T
E  E  A  E  R  N  E  L  A  D  T  T  E  N
T  G  B  T  N  M  O  R  T  I  E  E  L  A
E  N  R  A  C  O  E  R  N  T  L  M  T  D
L  I  A  O  R  H  R  I  H  O  A  G  R  R
L  R  E  I  G  R  M  V  R  C  N  B  A  A
E  E  R  O  A  R  U  E  E  I  T  P  M  G
C  P  M  N  E  N  D  L  N  H  D  U  R  E
N  A  I  O  I  N  P  O  E  T  C  R  C  R
O  I  O  C  A  N  O  Z  K  I  T  P  B  S
I  D  N  B  N  A  Z  T  N  A  H  C  B  C
L  R  I  I  L  E  H  C  U  O  B  U  A  C
N  I  S  B  N  O  Z  A  L  B  M  E  R  T
```

Find 67 biblical characters, and reveal a well-known letter sequence.

```
R S U E A H C C A Z H C E L E M I B A T
G A A B C T D B Z E M R A N T L L V F T
S A Z A D O K E A G A N E I M I I E E O
B U M Z E B U L O N D L L U N I T J V L
I P I A E A H A B R A E D U B S R U A E
R H A R L N I C E D I H S O I E I I S H
E Y J U A I D W G R S K A T R S N L A L
H D H M L D E A U N R U P I H C A L A M
C K U T O U M L H P H A L H N I A I Q S
A E K J O Y A E R C B A Z I I A R S A I
N P R O R M A S S E V A L Z H L H A S H
N E A A T N I H H H N B R E A P E P M O
E Z M S B A A T W R A O E T S H O M E N
S I J H H E N T E E U C C N I U S E O Z
A H A S V H L H A W H X H H Y M H L H N
M C I P O N T I U S P I L A T E A T E T
U L R J U S Z S E N R E F O L O H E E B
E E U A E A E S O H A I K E D E Z B U M
L M S B A R T H O L O M E W M O A B O S
L E H C A R U T H T A H P A H S O H E J
```

Q219   Power Puzzle★★★   A215

For this puzzle and the five that follow you will probably need a calculator or mathematical tables.

Replace the letters using the digits 1 to 9 inclusive. Each letter represents a different digit. A, D, E and F are even numbers.

$$A\ C\ I\ D = B^F + E^F + G^F = H^F + I^F + D^F$$

Q220   Power Puzzle★★★   A233

ABCDEFGF is an 8-digit number. The digits 1 and 9 do not appear. Even numbers appear in ascending order, odd numbers in descending order. What are A, B, C, D, E, F and G equal to?

$$A\ B\ C\ D\ E\ F\ G\ F = A^E + B^E + C^E + D^E + E^E + F^E + G^E + F^E$$

Q221   Power Puzzle★★★★   A188

ABCDEFGCC is a 9-digit number. The numbers 1, 2 and 6 do not appear. The odd numbers 3, 5, 7 and 9 appear in ascending order. What are A, B, C, D, E, F and G equal to?

$$A\ B\ C\ D\ E\ F\ G\ C\ C = A^A + B^B + C^C + D^D + E^E + F^F + G^G + C^C + C^C$$

Q222 Power Puzzle★★★★ A167

ABB, ACD, AED, FBE and CEA are 3-digit numbers. Each letter has been replaced by a different number. What are A, B, C, D, E, F and G equal to?

$A\ B\ B = A^C + G^C + C^C + F^C$

$A\ C\ D = A^A + C^G + D^C$

$A\ E\ D = A^G + E^G + D^C$

$F\ B\ E = F^C + B^C + E^C$

$C\ E\ A = C^C + E^C + A^C$

Q223 The Square Cube★★★★ A252

Find a number whose square and cube between them use all the digits from 0 to 9 inclusive.

Q224 Power Property★★★★★ A179

Replace the letters using the digits 1 to 9 inclusive. Each letter represents a different digit. F, G, H and I are odd numbers. When complete, 6-figure numbers with the same property, which no other 6-figure numbers possess, will be revealed.

$G\ B\ I,\ G\ B\ E = E\ D\ B^D$

$A\ D\ B;\ A\ D\ F = H\ D\ H^D$

$H\ G\ A,\ H\ G\ C = B\ E\ C^D$

Q225 Cryptogram Quotation*** A204

This puzzle and the two that follow are straightforward
cyptograms where one letter of the alphabet has been
replaced by another.

Decode the following:

'LIH LRQH IMF ZDQH,' LIH XMKPVF FMRY,

'LD LMKS DT QMWB LIRWEF;

DT FIDHF—MWY FIRJF—
MWY FHMKRWE XMN—

DT ZMAAMEHF—MWY SRWEF—

MWY XIB LIH FHM RF ADRKRWE IDL—

MWY XIHLIHP JREF IMGH XRWEF.'

KHXRF ZMPPDKK

Q226 Cryptogram Rhyme*** A223

Decode the following:

YKH DIC, YKH VOZZ, YKH
KHIWHRZT YEURL,

IRX RHMY YKH PDIV, YKH ZUJR LKURHL,

YKH WUDQUR, IRX YKH LPIZHL,

YKH LPJDFUJR, IDPKHD, IRX KH-QJIY,

YKH CIR YKIY VHIDL YKH EIYHDURQ-FJY,

IRX BULK EUYK QZUYYHDURQ YIUZL.

(LUQRL JB YKH NJXUIP.)

Q227   Cryptogram Limerick***   A197

Decode the following:

MTPSP'D K YAIXPSWRN WKUCNL GKNNPX
DMPCI

MTPSP'D BPSM KIX MTPSP'D PQQ KIX
MTPSP'D PCI;

BPSM'D QAPUD KSP ZRIH,

PQQ'D DMKMRPD KSP ORIH,

KIX IA AIP GKI RIXPSDMKIX PCI.

(BPSMSRXP DMPCI, OKGAZ PQDMPCI,
KNZPSM PCIDMPCI.)

Q228   Double Quote***   A211

Two quotations have been mixed up below. All the letters
of both quotations are in the correct order. See if you can
unscramble the two quotations, the authors of which have
something in common.

WHGAITVIESOUURSTATSHEKTOTOOMAL

ASKEBARNIDTWAIENAFWITICOLULNFTRI

YNFOIRSHHERTOEHSTEOLJIVEOIBN

Q229 Code One**** A170

Decode the following message:

15,1,6,36 78,15,153,153,15,171 45,105 210,36,45,190

91,15,190,190,1,28,15 36,1,190 3,15,15,105

171,15,136,78,1,6,15,10 3,325 210,36,15

210,171,45,1,105,28,231,78,1,171 105,231,91,3,15,171

6,120,171,171,15,190,136,120,105,10,45,105,28 210,120

45,210,190 136,120,190,45,210,45,120,105 45,105

210,36,15 1,78,136,36,1,3,15,210.

Replace each of the letters in the following two sentences with another letter to reveal something which may help you solve a clue sometime. One of the letters has already been placed in a grid for you.

A	B	C	D	E	F	G	H	I	J	K	L	M	N	O	P	Q	R	S	T	U	V	W	X	Y	Z
						R																			

YAWC ITPYRCR OGNIN NUP AN IFLAH

_____ _____ _____ ___ __ _____

REHTOEH TOTSDNO PSE RYLNO, EULC

_____ _____ ___ _____ ____

EHTFOF LAHENOO TLLE WGNITAL ERE

_____ _____ ____ _____ ___

LIHW, REWSN AEHTTA HTSNRAWT I,

_____ _____ _____ _____ _

TCEFFENI. GNINA EMELBUODA OTN

_____ _____ _____ ___

OITNETT AWARDO TSEHSI WDNAT

_____ _____ _____ _____

NELOVEN EBGNIL EEFSI RETT ESEL ZZU

_____ _____ ____ ____ ____ ___

PEHTNEH WDESU SIKRAMNO ITS EUQA,

_____ _____ _____ ___ ____

SEUL CDROW SSORCG NITT ESNEHW

____ _____ _____ ____ _____

154

Q231   Inner Word Square★   A163

This puzzle and the five that follow are based on word squares. These are squares made up of words of equal length that read both horizontally and vertically. Mostly the words are the same in both directions but sometimes the horizontal and vertical ones differ.

Place the remaining 18 letters into the grid to form a 5 × 5 word square, the centre of which is a 3 × 3 word square.

A   A   A   A   C   C   D   E   E   E   H   N   O   R
R   R   T   W

C				H
			R	
T		P		
				O
	E			

Q232   Word Square Links★★★   A149

Place the pairs of letters into the grid on page 156 to form five 4 × 4 word squares. The four outer squares overlap the centre square by one letter; the four letters being P, E, E and Y. You may only place one pair of letters in each rectangle, and the first letter of each pair must be placed to the left of the second letter if you place the pair in a horizontal rectangle, and above the second letter if placed in a vertical rectangle. Each square reads the same down as across.

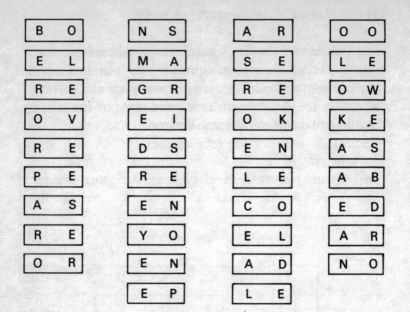

Q233 Word Squares*** A248

Place the blocks of three letters into the spaces in the large square to form four word squares. Each contains five 5-letter words, and reads the same down as across. There are 20 different 5-letter words in all, and some blocks overlap two word squares. A thicker horizontal line and a dotted vertical line separate the four squares.

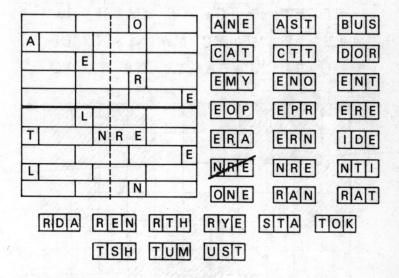

Q234 All Square** A243

Fit the nine squares together to form a word square containing six 6-letter words.

RE	TE	ER	TA	RT	CI	ES	TE	GA
TR	ER	SE	EL	ER	IB	RE	AL	AV

157

Q235 Word Square Grid**** A227

Place the pairs of letters in the grid to complete the cross-word and form eight overlapping word squares. The first letter in each pair should be placed above the second letter if the two letters are entered vertically.

AD AK AM AP AY EE EF ER

ET EW FF GA GE HA IP JA

LE LY ME ME MO NE NI OD

OD RA RI TA TA WR YA YO

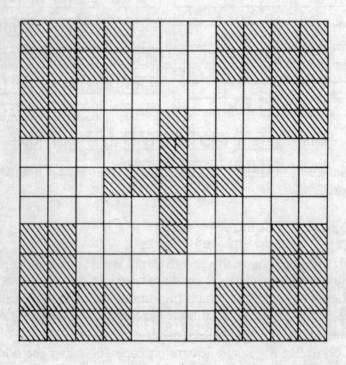

Q236   Word Cube****   A220

Place the list of 18 letters into the centre and bottom grids to form two three by three word squares. Then place all three grids together to form a cube so that a total of 18 different 3-letter words are formed by reading any three letters in a straight line; *e.g.* when the three grids are placed on top of each other to form a cube, the top left-hand square of the top grid, the centre square of the centre grid and the bottom right-hand square of the bottom grid will form a straight line of three letters. Diagonal words in the word squares also count.

A A A E E E E E E N R R
T W W Y

| TOP | CENTRE | BOTTOM |

TOP

A	S	A
S	E	C
A	C	E

CENTRE

BOTTOM

(Not all straight lines of three letters have to form a 3-letter word.)

Q237   Magic Square*   A174

This puzzle and the next eight are based on magic squares. These are squares in which the sum of the numbers in all the rows, columns and both diagonals is the same. A number should only be used once.

Complete the magic square on page 160 using the odd numbers from 5-35 inclusive. When all the numbers have been entered, all columns, rows and both diagonals should total 80. Five numbers have been entered as a start.

159

17			23
7			
		25	5

Q238   Squares in Square**   A200

Place the remaining whole numbers from 2 to 17 inclusive
into the diagram. When complete, all columns, rows and
both diagonals should total 38. Also, each corner block of
four squares, the four centre squares and the four corner
squares should also total 38.

		15	
13			
			6
	4		

Q239 Magic Square Tiles*** A191

Place the 21 3-figure numbers into the grid, either vertically or horizontally. When complete, all the columns and rows must equal 45 when the numbers in them are added together.

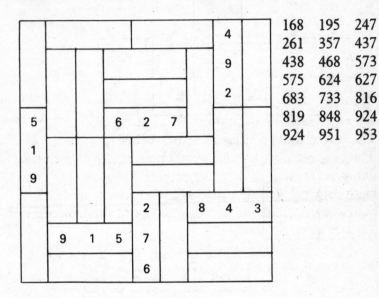

168	195	247
261	357	437
438	468	573
575	624	627
683	733	816
819	848	924
924	951	953

Q240 All the Fours*** A208

Fit the 14 pieces together to form a magic square. When complete, all columns, rows and both diagonals should total 444.

Fit the 18 pieces into the grid opposite to form a magic square. When complete, all rows, columns and both diagonals should total 175. Some pieces overlap each other at the joints between the squares.

e.g.

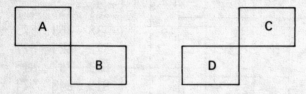

The pieces could overlap as shown below:

A	C
D	B

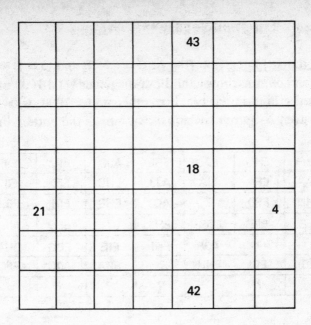

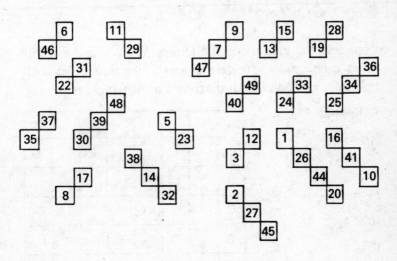

Q242   The Bottom Line***   A235

Given that J = O, G = E + A, B = C + I, and D = B − G, and all columns, rows and both diagonals total 1000 more than the highest triangular number under 1000, what are the seven 3-figure numbers missing from the bottom line?

EBF	EHG	EFG	EBE	AJD	EFJ	EIF
?	EFA	EIA	AJJ	EHC	EFI	EII
EHD	EFD	?	ACJ	EHB	EIH	EBH
EFE	EIE	EBB	EHJ	?	EBD	AJH
EIJ	?	AJB	EHI	EIG	EBG	EHA
EIC	EBI	EHH	?	EBA	AJG	EFC
?	?	?	?	?	?	?

Q243   Grid Zero****   A183

Complete the grid using the letters A, B, E and F eight times each, and the letters C and D 16 times each. All columns, rows and both diagonals must equal zero.

$A = +25.132$

$B = -A$

$C = \frac{1}{2}A$

$D = A - (6 \times E)$

$E = \frac{1}{2}C$

$F = ?$

A							C
			B		F		D
			A				
C			D				
C				E			
F							C
B							A
		C	C			E	

164

Q244 Magic Letter Square**** A160

Complete the grid so that all the columns, rows and both diagonals equal A, and the grid contains the letters K–Z four times each.

$A = (P \times T) + R$

$Z = 2 \times R$

$N = V/3$

$T = Y - (N + K)$

$U = S + L$

$(M \times Q) + O + K = W + X$

Total value of K – Z = 136

K							
						V	
	O						
				M			
							W
		X					
	Z						
			N				

Using the whole numbers from 1 to 64 inclusive, complete the four grids so that the columns, rows and both diagonals in A = 124, B = 128, C = 132 and D = 136. When all four grids are placed on top of each other, all 16 columns total 130. For example, 61 + 14 + 3 + 52 = 130. Twenty numbers have been entered for you.

A

61			
		41	
	21		
	57		01

B

14			62
	22		
		42	
02			

C

03	55		
47			
			19
		11	

D

52		48	
			56
12			
	20		

Q246   Clueless Crossword**   A164

Fit the letters into the blank crossword grid to form 48 different 3-letter words. The letters have been placed next to the row in which they fit. The letters have also been placed under the column in which they fit.

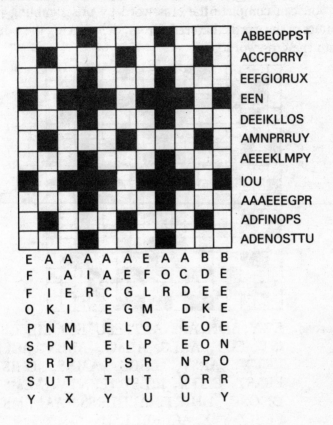

| | | | | | | | | | | ABBEOPPST |
| ACCFORRY |
| EEFGIORUX |
| EEN |
| DEEIKLLOS |
| AMNPRRUY |
| AEEEKLMPY |
| IOU |
| AAAEEEGPR |
| ADFINOPS |
| ADENOSTTU |

E	A	A	A	A	A	E	A	A	B	B
F	I	A	I	A	E	F	O	C	D	E
F	I	E	R	C	G	L	R	D	E	E
O	K	I		E	G	M		D	K	E
P	N	M		E	L	O		E	O	E
S	P	N		E	L	P		E	O	E
S	R	P		P	S	R		N	P	O
S	U	T		T	U	T		O	R	R
Y	X			T		Y		U	R	Y
Y				Y		U		U		Y

The following crossword has no clues, but you have the answers in front of you. Unfortunately, none of the answers are numbered, and the letters of the words that fit across the crossword have been arranged into alphabetical order. See if you can complete the crossword by unscrambling the letters of the words that read across, then placing the words into the crossword grid.

Across   EWY, ADN, APS, AET, ESU, ESS, EIL, CES, IST, EOT, AALS, ALMT, ABEN, ACEL, EETW, ARST, EHOS, AMRS, EHIST, EELST, EISTX, EILST, EENTV, AEMST, DNOSU, DHIRT, AEHLRSS, AAELMST, EEEIPRSTX, ACEFLLLSU.

Down   ECU, STY, NEW, COS, URE, PHI, ANE, AIL, ILL, ULE, EFT, ATE, STAR, NETT, BEAM, REST, SEAT, LESS, ELSE, ANEW, SLEET, TERMS, THEFT, SPICE, HASTE, DEALT, DREAM, LEAPS, ESCAPER, METRICS, VALENTINE, ALONGSIDE.

Q248   Three Too Many***   A151

Delete three of the letters in each square to reveal a cross-word with ten interlocking words.

YA UB	EH CO	RL NS	LW EA	RA VI	ZP MT	BC HE
AC BD		PY OA			LG FA	
PR US	NT OE	GM KS	EQ GU	HG MF	PU CH	BS TR
LJ UT		EJ FV		LA ZT		GI RO
GK QJ	IY MN	FD HT	PS ID	ES IA	PR YN	GI AU
	LU KY			QY JZ		BH CG
OK CB	SL TR	RI ED	KM LO	PR AE	IO JN	TE RG

169

The clues given for the crossword below are the answers in a coded form. Each digit of the clue represents two or three different letters of the alphabet as shown in the table below; *e.g.*:

(A) Across '3382', could be 'HIVE', derived from:
(G, H or I) + (G, H or I) + (V, W or X) + (D, E or F)
    H   +   I + V   +   E

Across
a 3382   d 2177265   g 1855   h 77562   i 1421826
k 22137   l 7578377   n 5333781713515   q 1337172
s 53779   t 6475132   u 73567   v 5513   w 1425257
x 2556

Down
a 317326353   b 8165373   c 282   d 2515761325257
e 7126731   f 25853   j 657   m 711772626   o 7211142
p 3233335   q 146   r 35762   u 712

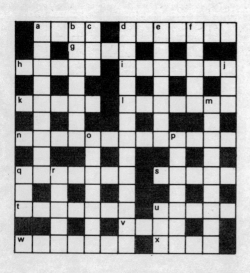

1	A	B	C
2	D	E	F
3	G	H	I
4	J	K	L
5	M	N	O
6	P	Q	R
7	S	T	U
8	V	W	X
9	Y	Z	–

Fit the 25 pieces together to form a symmetrical crossword.

	T	O			O			P	O	R		E	N	T
O	R				L	E			U			A		Y
	O			A	L			S	T	A		L	L	

	T	I
A		N
B	I	C

	E	T		E		U		H	O	S		O		A
		A		A		N			A			R		
E	F	L		T	O	T		A	T	E		A	R	R

U	C	H
S		E
E		A

H	R	A		S				L	E	S		T	O	P
		R		S	T	E				E		N		
E	A	C				N		D		I		E	R	O

D	A	L
	N	
	I	

E	S				T			T	I	O		B	L	E
S	S				E			I				O		W
		A		S	M	A		L	E			A	T	E

	G	
G	R	A
	E	

	U			N		C		D		H		L		
R	G	E		E	R	R		D	G	E			G	O
	B			A		O		Y		D		H		C

A	W	E
S		O
K	I	N

Fit the 50 pieces opposite together to form two crosswords, each of a symmetrical pattern.

Row 1:

P	R	E		A	L	D		T	S			H	U	L			A	
	O			L		O			H	A			M			P	R	O
A	B	O		A	M	P		L	Y			S	E	N			G	

Row 2:

	I	S		I	S	C		E		O			A	R		R	I	V
		E		N		C		R	E	R		E	L	M			D	
D	G	L		T		U			V			L	E			S		A

Row 3:

	N				H			W				S	S	S				I
A	T	E			Y	O			D	O		A				D	U	C
L		N		S		C		L				V	E			E		E

Row 4:

	S	C			L			T	I	C			N				B	L
	C			L	E	A		E		U		E	P	I			L	
C	H			O		N		M	O	R			A			S	E	

Row 5:

E	E	D			O			E	A	P		A		E		E	S	T
S		E			O	V		N		E		T						H
S	A	N		O	L	O		O	N	C		E	X	P		T		R

Row 6:

E				L	E	T		D		M		O	V	E		L	O	T
D	D	E			N			E				S		L		O		I
Y		A		A	S	S		S	A	L		E	W	E		C	A	R

Row 7:

T	U	D		O	P	I			H	E		K	N	O			T	
O		A				S		D	E			Y	O			N	U	R
P	A	R		R		A			A	D			B				N	

Row 8:

V	E	N				K		E		S		R		N		S		R
I		O		L	Y			R	D	E			A			T	R	U
E	R	T				S		Y		D		E	T	T		E		C

Row 9:

N		L		O	T	A		E		A		A	D	R		L		T
A	D	E		T		B		D	E	N		D		O		L		I
R				T	C	H				G		D	U	C		A	T	O

Row 10:

	Y			E		E		T		E		O	P	Y		E	V	E
N	E	R		T	E	N		E	R	O			L			A		A
	R				M				O			P	O	N		S	I	T

173

The crossword below has had all its letters replaced by numbers. Only nine different letters have been used in the crossword. Each has been replaced by a number from 0 to 8. Which letter does each of the nine numbers represent?

6		4	5	5	4	7	0	4	8	6		6	7	3
4	0	6	2		0			7		2		2		0
3		2		5	1	3		2	3	6	1	6	6	1
6	7	8	1	4		4		0		1		4		4
		4		0	4	5	5	7	1		3	0	4	8
4	0	0	2	6	6	1	1		8	7	0			
	7		5		6		3		6		7	8	6	2
	8		3	2	4	5	6	0	7	8	1		1	
5	2	0	7		7		7		6		8		1	
		8	2	8		2	7	0	5	6	2	8	1	
0	7	8	1		6	7	8	5	1	0		0		
4		7		8		8		0		7	0	1	4	0
6	2	1	8	4	7	0		1	4	6		4		4
1		3		8		1			0		2	6	7	3
8	1	1		4	8	6	7	3	0	7	8	1		1

Fit the 75 pieces together to form three crosswords, each of symmetrical pattern.

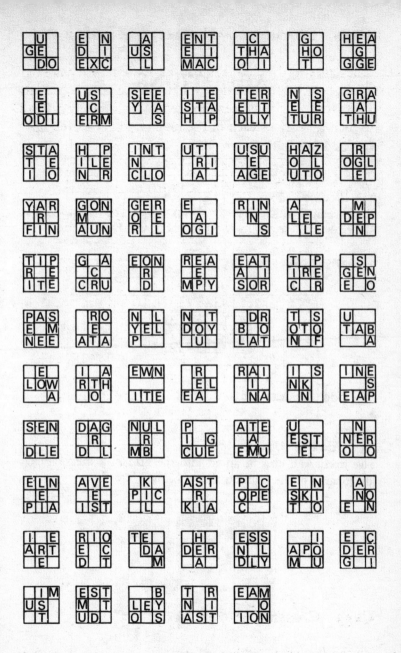

175

SOLUTIONS

A1   Odd One Out   Q15
Cube C.

A2   Blocked   Q29
Blocks rotated anticlockwise = A1, A3, B3, B5, C1, D2, D3, E5;
Blocks rotated clockwise = A5, B2, C2, C4, D4, E1, E4.

A3   Mix Up Square   Q45

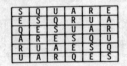

A4   Odd One Out   Q63
A.

A5   Grid Fill   Q72
The words can also be fitted into the grid in a mirror image
(diagonally) of the solution shown below.

A6   Laser Maze   Q89
1. X squares = B3, G10, I7;
2. Y squares = A8, B1, C8, D1, H3;
3. Z squares = A7, C1, C5, C7, F8, G3, H2, J5.

A7   Blocked   Q109
Blocks rotated anticlockwise = A1, B2, C4, D3, E5;
Blocks rotated clockwise = A4, B5, C1, D2, E3;
Blocks rotated 180° = A3, C3, D5, E1.

A8   Blocked   Q117
Blocks rotated anticlockwise = A1, A2, A3, C3, D1;
Blocks rotated clockwise = B2, B3, C4, D2, D5;
Blocks rotated 180° = B4, C5, D3, E1, E4, E5.

A9   Letter Boxes   Q133

H	F	D	G	C	B	E	I	J	A
A	C	I	D	G	E	B	H	F	J
G	J	C	H	F	I	A	D	E	B
I	G	H	C	B	D	J	F	A	E
B	H	F	J	A	G	D	E	I	C
D	A	J	B	E	F	I	C	G	H
J	I	E	F	H	C	G	A	B	D
E	B	A	I	D	H	F	J	C	G
C	E	B	A	I	J	H	G	D	F
F	D	G	E	J	A	C	B	H	I

A10 Grid Fill Q4

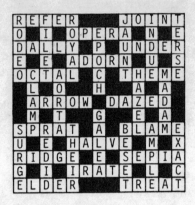

A11 The Mad Hatter Q25

The Mad Hatter wore the top hat on Friday and the fez is orange.
The full solution is as follows:

Monday –	Stetson –	Blue
Tuesday –	Bowler hat –	Red
Wednesday –	Trilby –	Green
Thursday –	Cap –	Yellow
Friday –	Top hat –	White
Saturday –	Fez –	Orange
Sunday –	Sombrero –	Black

A12 Double Wordsquare Q36

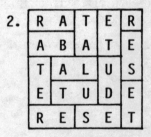

A13 What Next? Q55

B is the next most appropriate square.

Each square is divided into four smaller squares of equal size. In the centre of each of these smaller squares is another square which does not change. There are various circles and lines surrounding each of these squares that don't change, which, as the sequence progresses, rotate around the square in a clockwise direction. The various lines and circles rotate at different speeds. They rotate twice the distance in the upper right-hand square as they do in the upper left-hand square, and twice the distance in the lower right-hand square as they do in the upper right-hand square. Finally, they rotate twice the distance in the lower left-hand square as they do in the lower right-hand square.

A14 Number Fill Q70

12	10	1	8	3	1	3
7	2	7	12	7	10	7
4	10	5	9	3	1	3
11	2	8	■	11	5	6
4	5	9	12	2	9	11
12	10	2	5	8	1	6
4	6	8	11	6	9	4

A15 Clockwork Q87
The letters around the numbers given in brackets were rotated in the following order and direction:

(4) – 90° anticlockwise;
(3) – 90° anticlockwise;
(2) – 90° clockwise;
(1) – 90° clockwise;
(2) – 90° clockwise;
(3) – 180°;
(4) – 90° anticlockwise.

A16 Odd One Out Q93
C.

A17 Chessboard Q115

Each letter has been moved one square to the right and two squares down. Where the letter would move off the grid, the grid has been treated as continuous.

S	E	K	V	H
X	J	P	B	M
D	O	U	G	R
I	T	A	L	W
N	Y	F	Q	C

A18 Birthday Boys Q127

Alan—cassette tape;
Barry—record token;
Carl—video cassette tape;
David—compact disc.

A19 3D Movement Q142

Direction	Distance in cubes
Right	Two
Down	One
Left	Two
Down	One
Forward	Two
Up	Two
Right	One
Backwards	One
Left	One
Down	One
Right	Two
Up	One
Forward	One
Down	Two
Backwards	Two
Left	One
Forward	Two
Up	One

A20 Logic Box Q10

```
H C A
B G E
F I D
```

A21 Logic Box Q38

```
E I B
A G D
H C F
```

A22 Clockwork Q69

The letters around the numbers given in brackets were rotated in the following order and direction:

(1) – 180°;
(2) – 180°;
(4) – 90° anticlockwise;
(3) – 180°;
(2) – 90° anticlockwise;
(3) – 90° clockwise;
(4) – 90° clockwise.

The third rotation shown above could take place first without any effect on the outcome, as there is no further effect until the fourth rotation which then alters the positions of the letters moved by the first three rotations.

A23 Cross Check Q97

Number 4. The number of triangles increase by one vertically and decrease by one horizontally. The circles increase by one horizontally and decrease by one vertically.

A24 Odd One Out Q122

Number 2 is the odd one out. The remaining four figures are all different views of the same solid figure. (Two 'pyramids' attached at the base.)

A25　Auntie Christmas　Q28

Auntie Carol will get the slippers. (Auntie Sheila will get the voucher, Auntie Mary the chocolates and Auntie Joan the flowers.)

A26　Letter Boxes　Q58

F	H	J	G	D	C	I	A	B	E
G	C	B	D	A	H	E	I	F	J
B	I	D	H	E	J	A	G	C	F
E	D	I	A	F	G	J	B	H	C
D	A	C	F	H	B	G	E	J	I
C	E	H	J	B	A	F	D	I	G
J	F	A	I	G	E	C	H	D	B
H	J	F	E	I	D	B	C	G	A
I	G	E	B	C	F	D	J	A	H
A	B	G	C	J	I	H	F	E	D

A27　Logic Box　Q85

I	B	P	E
O	F	A	N
C	L	G	K
H	J	M	D

A28　Block Cut　Q116

A29　What Next?　Q135

B. The hexagon is divided into three pairs of triangles. Firstly, at each stage, the hexagon rotates 60° clockwise about its centre. Secondly, a change takes place in the position of the dots in the pairs of triangles at each stage.

1. Pair one – the two triangles containing two dots each. The dots appear in two corners of the triangles with the empty corner moving in a clockwise direction in one triangle and an anticlockwise direction in the other triangle.

2. Pair two – one pair of triangles containing a single dot each. They start with one dot in the centre of the face common with the hexagon and a dot in the corner of the triangle nearest the centre of the hexagon. Each dot moves in the following sequence; outside edge, centre, and centre corner of the triangle. One step being taken each rotation of the hexagon. Both dots only being in the same position of the sequence when they are in the centre of their respective triangles.

3. Pair three – the remaining two triangles. The dots in the triangles move clockwise in one triangle and anticlockwise in the other triangle. Both move one half the distance of one side of the triangle each time the hexagon rotates 60°.

A30   Paint-by-Numbers   Q1
Sections 5 and 7.

A31   Square Cut   Q30

A32   Wordsquares   Q64

1. HOME	2. LIMP	3. DOTE	4. TEAM
OPEN	IDEA	ORAL	EDGE
MEMO	MEAL	TASS	AGAR
ENOW	PALE	ELSE	MERE

A33   Father Unlike Son   Q92
Plumber.

A34 Grid Fill Q118

The words can also be fitted into the grid in a mirror image (diagonally) of the solution shown below.

A35 Logicalympics – The Beginning Q144

The teams entered the stadium in the following order:

1. Hungary
2. Austria
3. Brazil
4. Spain
5. Turkey
6. Great Britain
7. Romania
8. Finland
9. Mexico
10. Germany
11. Ethiopia
12. India
13. Canada
14. Algeria
15. New Zealand
16. Australia
17. Norway
18. France
19. Portugal
20. Greece
21. Japan
22. Sweden
23. Venezuela
24. China
25. Denmark
26. USA

A36 Odd Block Out Q18

4. The remaining seven blocks are all different views of the same block.

A37 Grid Fill Q47

The words can also be fitted into the grid in a mirror image (diagonally) of the solution below.

R	I	N	S	E	■	■	S	P	E	N	T
O	■	O	■	V	I	S	I	T	■	M	■	A
O	P	I	N	E	■	O	■	A	M	E	N	T
S	■	S	■	N	E	W	E	L	■	N	■	E
T	R	E	A	T	■	E	■	E	L	D	E	R
■	E	■	T	■	■	R	■	I	■	V
■	V	I	L	L	A	■	V	E	N	U	E
■	U	■	A	■	■	C	■	E	■	N
Y	E	A	S	T	■	A	■	A	R	I	S	E
O	■	L	■	H	A	R	E	M	■	■	X
D	O	L	C	E	■	O	■	O	K	A	P	I
E	■	O	■	I	D	L	E	R	■	G	■	L
L	A	T	E	R	■	■	■	T	H	E	M	E

A38 Gruffs Q76

1. Retriever
2. Bull Terrier
3. Whippet
4. Great Dane
5. Chow
6. Bulldog
7. Yorkshire Terrier
8. King Charles Spaniel
9. Greyhound
10. Chihuahua
11. Dachshund
12. Spaniel
13. Dalmatian
14. Afghan Hound
15. Beagle
16. Bull Mastiff
17. Foxhound
18. Labrador
19. Poodle
20. Collie
21. Pug
22. St Bernard
23. Griffon
24. Sheepdog
25. Alsatian
26. Dobermann Pinscher

A39 Mix Up Squarebox Q106

B	S	O	U	Q	R	A	E	X
U	E	X	S	A	B	R	O	Q
R	A	Q	E	X	O	B	S	U
Q	R	A	X	O	E	U	B	S
O	B	S	Q	R	U	X	A	E
X	U	E	A	B	S	Q	R	O
E	X	U	B	S	A	O	Q	R
A	Q	R	O	E	X	S	U	B
S	O	B	R	U	Q	E	X	A

A40   Which Way Next?   Q131
C = 1; H = 2; A = 3; D = 4; F = 5; B = 6; E = 7; G = 8.

There is a quick way of solving the puzzle rather than trying each different type of arrow in place of each letter. You must always stay in the grid boundary, therefore if any of the letters in the top row replaced arrows numbered 1, 2 or 8 this would not be the case. Therefore, letters A, B, D and E did not replace arrows numbered 1, 2 and 8. Using the same principle, letters B, C and G could not replace arrows 2, 3, or 4, letters A, C, E and H could not replace arrows 4, 5, or 6, and letters A, C, D, F and H could not replace arrows 6, 7 or 8. Also, letter C could not replace arrow 5 as this would return you to the square containing one dot, as would the letter H if it had replaced arrow number 7. Given the above information you only have to refer to the grid to work out which arrows were replaced by the letters D and F.

A41   Who's Who?   Q2
Smith. Statements 1 and 3 are false.

A42   Before or Not Before?   Q27
1. Titus Andronicus
2. Two Gentlemen of Verona
3. Romeo and Juliet
4. As You Like It
5. Julius Caesar
6. Merry Wives of Windsor
7. The Winter's Tale
8. Measure for Measure
9. All's Well That Ends Well
10. Timon of Athens
11. Love's Labour's Lost
12. Troilus and Cressida
13. Much Ado About Nothing
14. The Taming of the Shrew
15. The Merchant of Venice
16. Hamlet
17. Antony and Cleopatra
18. The Tempest
19. The Comedy of Errors
20. King John
21. Twelfth Night
22. Coriolanus
23. Macbeth
24. Cymbeline
25. A Midsummer Night's Dream

A43   Odd One Out   Q40
B.

A44 Grouping Q56

Group 1. The letter J has no vertical or horizontal symmetry. The letters in group 2 are symmetrical about the horizontal axis, the letter in group 3 is symmetrical about the vertical axis and the letters in group 4 are symmetrical about the vertical and the horizontal axis.

A45 Mix Up Squared Q67

S	Q	U	A	R	E	D
R	A	E	S	D	Q	U
D	S	Q	R	A	U	E
A	D	S	E	U	R	Q
U	E	R	Q	S	D	A
E	R	D	U	Q	A	S
Q	U	A	D	E	S	R

A46 Mix Up Squarely Q88

S	Q	U	A	R	E	L	Y
R	L	Y	E	U	Q	A	S
Q	S	A	U	L	Y	R	E
L	R	E	Y	A	S	U	Q
Y	E	R	L	S	A	Q	U
U	A	S	Q	Y	L	E	R
E	Y	L	R	Q	U	S	A
A	U	Q	S	E	R	Y	L

A47 Logicalympics – Swimming Q98

Event	Gold medal	Silver medal	Bronze medal
100 m freestyle	USA	GB	C
100 m backstroke	USA	G	G
100 m breastroke	GB	C	USA
100 m butterfly	G	GB	GB
200 m freestyle	G	USA	G
200 m backstroke	GB	USA	USA
200 m breaststroke	C	G	GB .
200 m butterfly	C	C	C

A48 Connection Q123

3. In each of the five rows of smaller squares, the square which is completely filled has exchanged places with one of the remaining four squares in the same row, except the fourth row from the top of the square, which remains the same.

A49 Mix Up Four Hundred Q145

1	2	3	4	5	6	7	8	9	10	11	12	13	14	15	16	17	18	19	20
2	18	1	6	3	13	20	14	15	12	17	11	7	19	8	10	9	16	4	5
3	20	4	12	13	16	18	15	1	9	19	10	6	17	5	8	7	2	14	11
4	3	13	14	11	12	6	5	7	8	10	9	16	15	1	2	18	19	20	17
5	15	19	11	7	18	3	9	2	17	6	16	4	10	20	14	13	1	8	12
6	8	5	17	18	4	1	3	19	16	13	15	10	12	9	20	14	11	7	2
7	10	8	18	19	1	15	2	20	13	3	14	11	6	12	17	4	5	9	16
8	14	17	5	9	20	2	12	16	19	7	13	1	11	18	4	3	15	10	6
9	11	10	19	20	15	14	16	17	3	2	4	5	7	6	18	1	8	12	13
10	4	20	8	12	19	16	6	13	18	9	3	15	5	17	1	2	14	11	7
11	1	18	10	6	17	13	7	3	20	12	2	14	8	19	15	16	4	5	9
12	5	11	20	17	14	4	13	18	2	16	1	8	9	7	19	15	10	6	3
13	17	14	9	16	2	19	1	4	7	20	8	12	18	11	5	6	3	15	10
14	13	16	15	10	9	12	11	6	5	8	7	2	1	4	3	20	17	18	19
15	16	2	1	8	7	9	10	12	11	5	6	3	4	14	13	19	20	17	18
16	19	15	7	2	3	17	4	14	6	18	5	9	20	10	11	12	13	1	8
17	12	9	3	15	5	8	18	10	4	1	19	20	13	16	6	11	7	2	14
18	6	12	2	14	8	10	19	11	1	15	20	17	3	13	7	5	9	16	4
19	9	7	13	1	11	5	20	8	14	4	17	18	16	2	12	10	6	3	15
20	7	6	16	4	10	11	17	5	15	14	18	19	2	3	9	8	12	13	1

A50 Square Cut Q13

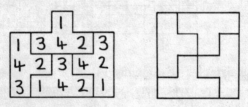

A51 Every Which Way Q22

1	2	3	4	5
4	5	1	2	3
2	3	4	5	1
5	1	2	3	4
3	4	5	1	2

1	2	3	4	5
3	4	5	1	2
5	1	2	3	4
2	3	4	5	1
4	5	1	2	3

A52 Laser Maze Q41
1. X squares = B2, B10, C10, J9;
2. Y squares = B4, C2, D4, E2, H2, H6, H9;
3. Z squares = A2, D5, I6.

A53 Coin Puzzle Q52
Place coin number 10 on top of coin number 5.

A54 Blocked Q84
Blocks rotated clockwise = A1, A3, A4, B1, B2, B4, B5, D2, E3, E5;
Blocks rotated anticlockwise = A5, C2, C3, C4, C5, D1, D3, D4, E1, E2.

A55 What Colour Next? Q90
My next-door neighbour painted his fence the following colours in the following order: Orange, Burgundy, Navy Blue, Indigo, Lavender, Olive Green, Violet, White, Turquoise, Lemon, Emerald Green, Sky Blue, Hazel Brown, Coal Black, Yellow, Mauve, Creamy White, Jade Green, Pitch Black, Fawn, Oxford Blue, Sea Blue, Purple, Primrose, Ruby Red and Red.

A56 Consider Q71
Diagram 5. All of the other diagrams consist of four shapes, each of which contains two dots. One dot is common to only the shape itself, the other dot is common to all four of the shapes.

A57 What Next? Q99
D. The pentagon contains six sections which alternate between black and white each time the pentagon rotates 72° clockwise. Five of the six sections within the pentagon have one side which is common to both the section and the pentagon. In pentagon number one, the two uppermost sections contain a black dot, as does the remaining white section. Each time the pentagon rotates 72° clockwise, all three dots rotate in an anticlockwise direction to the section which has one side common with the pentagon, two sides before the section the dot was previously in. The dots then change to the opposite colour of the section they are in.

D	O	E	L
J	P	F	C
I	G	K	B
M	A	H	N

A59   Clockwork Links   Q134

The letters around the numbers given in brackets were rotated in the following order and direction:

(3) – 90° clockwise;
(1) – 90° clockwise;
(3) – 180°;
(4) – 90° anticlockwise;
(2) – 90° anticlockwise;
(1) – 180°;
(2) – 90° clockwise;
(4) – 180°.

From this I get:

A	O	Q	N	K
D	1	B	2	H
E	F	I	R	S
J	3	T	4	L
C	G	U	P	M

A60   Odd One Out   Q141
B.

A61   Card Sharp   Q3
E = C; F = A; G = D; H = B. As E did not appear in Row 2, it must be on the other side of A or C, and, as A had already been in the position where E is, C must be on the other side of E. As F did not appear in Row 2, the other side must show A or C, and, as C is on the other side to E, A must be on the other side of F. D must therefore be on the other side of G because, of the two positions remaining, D has already been in the position where H is. This leaves B on the other side of H.

A62   Logic Box   Q23

```
F D G
I A C
B H E
```

A63   The Animals Went In Which Way?   Q44
The animals went into the Ark in the following order:

1. Otters
2. Elephants
3. Beavers
4. Lions
5. Tigers
6. Rabbits
7. Ducks
8. Doves
9. Goats
10. Pigs
11. Snakes
12. Foxes
13. Badgers
14. Horses
15. Donkeys
16. Mice
17. Leopards
18. Squirrels
19. Monkeys
20. Swans
21. Chickens
22. Sheep
23. Peacocks
24. Geese
25. Penguins
26. Spiders

A64   Jack of All Trades   Q62

1. Journalist
2. Signwriter
3. Cartoonist
4. Undertaker
5. Illustrator
6. Postmaster
7. Pawnbroker
8. Upholsterer
9. Ringmaster
10. Newscaster
11. Programmer
12. Fishmonger
13. Chargehand
14. Blacksmith
15. Escapologist
16. Greengrocer
17. Piano-tuner
18. Lumberjack
19. Woodcarver
20. Interpreter
21. Compositor
22. Taxi-driver
23. Roadsweeper
24. Electrician
25. Gamekeeper
26. Scene-shifter

A65   Logic Box   Q80

```
B D H
I C E
G F A
```

A66 Sparky Q107

Time	Job	Number of house
9.00 a.m.	Mend vacuum cleaner	27
10.00 a.m.	Mend dishwasher	51
11.00 a.m.	Mend fridge motor	52
12.00 noon	Install cooker point	14
2.00 p.m.	Install light in alcove	9
3.00 p.m.	Mend electric shower	13
4.00 p.m.	Mend broken socket	31
5.00 p.m.	Install wall lights	43

A67 The Host Q124
J was the host.

A68 Grid Fill – Numbers Q143
The numbers can also be fitted into the grid in a mirror image (diagonally) of the solution shown below.

A69 Every Which Way Q5

1	2	3	4
3	4	1	2
4	3	2	1
2	1	4	3

1	2	3	4
4	3	2	1
2	1	4	3
3	4	1	2

A70 Number Fill Q20

5	3	7	9	4	1
9	1	8	2	8	3
2	4	3	6	4	6
5	8	7	5	1	7
9	1	2	9	2	6
5	8	7	6	4	3

A71 Number Pyramid Q34

A = 8; B = 6; C = 9; D = 7; E = 3; F = 9. The pyramid contains the numbers one to nine as follows: one 1, two 2s, three 3s, four 4s, five 5s, six 6s, seven 7s, eight 8s and nine 9s. When complete, no two adjoining rectangles contain the same number.

A72 Number Fill Q51

4	7	9	5	6	1
8	2	1	2	7	3
4	5	6	5	8	4
7	2	9	2	1	3
8	1	6	5	8	4
9	7	9	3	6	3

A73 Blocked Q65

Blocks rotated anticlockwise = A1, C1, D3, E2.
Blocks rotated clockwise = B1, B2, D1, D4, E5.
Blocks rotated 180° = A5, B3, C3, D5.

A74 Connection Q86

5. The large square contains 16 smaller squares which have been grouped into four squares of four, each group forming another square, and have been rotated clockwise or anticlockwise about the centre of each group. The upper left and lower right groups have been rotated clockwise, the upper right and lower left groups have been rotated anticlockwise.

A75 Square Cut Q95

M	C	K	E	M	K	I	J
I	I	O	E	L	B	G	G
N	K	J	E	H	B	H	L
P	B	G	A	A	D	P	E
F	J	B	A	A	D	N	G
F	N	D	I	F	D	O	N
P	F	H	C	O	L	C	P
O	M	H	C	L	J	K	M

A76 Odd One Out Q110
C.

A77 Logic Cube Q125

TOP LAYER: BACK

J	S	A
Z	K	I
B	W	L

FRONT

MIDDLE LAYER: BACK

C	M	T
Q	G	X
N	U	D

FRONT

BOTTOM LAYER   BACK

E	P	H
V	@	Y
O	F	R

FRONT

A78 Laser Maze Q138
1. X squares = C1, E8, F3, F4, F8, H3, H9, I9;
2. Y squares = B6, E3, H2, H5, I3, I6, J4;
3. Z squares = A6, B3, B9, C6, E1.

194

A79 Odd Ones Out Q26

Cubes numbered 2, 5 and 7 cannot be formed from the flattened cube shown.

A80 Laser Maze Q7

1. X squares = A9, D8, E4, G10, J2;
2. Y squares = C2, C4, F8, G8, H6, I7;
3. Z squares = A4, E2, I2.

A81 Monarch E Q39

The solution is historically correct. The years which the monarchs reigned over England are included in the solution below.

Egbert	827 to	839
Ethelwulf	839	858
Ethelbald	858	860
Ethelbert	860	865
Ethelred	865	871
Edward the Elder	899	924
Edmund	939	946
Edred	946	955
Edwig	955	959
Edgar	959	975
Edward the Martyr	975	978
Ethelred the Unready	978	1016
Edmund Ironside	1016	1016
Edward the Confessor	1042	1066
Edward I (35 years)	1272	1307
Edward II (20 years)	1307	1327 (Deposed)
Edward III (10 years)	1327	1377
Edward IV (22 years)	1461	1483
Edward V (1 year)	1483	1483
Edward VI (6 years)	1547	1553
Elizabeth I	1558	1603
Edward VII (9 years)	1901	1910
Edward VIII (abdicated)	1936	1936
Elizabeth II	1952 to date.	

A82 Age Old Question Q57

1. Harry
2. Leonard
3. Bill
4. Jimmy
5. Tom
6. Eddie
7. Kevin
8. Fred
9. Martin
10. George
11. Simon
12. Ian
13. Colin
14. Arthur
15. Paul
16. Matthew
17. Neil
18. Frank
19. Philip
20. Michael
21. John
22. Keith
23. Barry
24. Robert
25. Dave
26. Joe

A83 Square Cut Q74

A84 Wordsquares Q82

1. MADE
   AMEN
   DEMO
   ENOW

2. MANE
   AREA
   NEAR
   EARN

3. OMEN
   MORE
   ERNE
   NEED

4. DAME
   AGED
   MERE
   EDEN

A85 Number Fill Q96

1	9	15	11	8	3	8	12
6	14	5	1	6	2	5	6
12	11	■	11	12	■	8	12
1	7	5	7	14	2	7	6
13	9	2	1	8	3	9	13
10	4	■	11	15	■	7	10
13	3	5	14	2	3	9	13
10	4	15	4	15	4	14	10

196

A86 Post Problem Q103

A87 Nine by Four Q114

	A	B	C	D	E	F
1	9	7	4	2	9	3
2	3	8	6	1	6	8
3	9	2	4	3	5	1
4	1	6	1	7	2	7
5	8	4	2	4	6	3
6	9	5	8	5	7	5

A88 Combination Q128
K, H, B, C, E, A, D, F, G, I, J.

A89 Housing Problem Q139

1 = L	7 = P	13 = G
2 = D	8 = I	14 = E
3 = K	9 = A	15 = O
4 = Q	10 = M	16 = F
5 = B	11 = C	17 = H
6 = J	12 = N	

A90 Stationary Stationery Q8
George carried the three small parcels. Fred carried the two medium-sized parcels. Arthur carried the large parcel.

A91 Grid Fill Q24

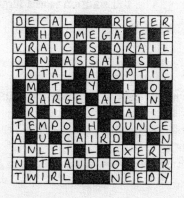

A92 Colour Cube Q33

The smaller cubes can form a larger cube as described if placed in the following positions:

Top layer

23	26	10
17	6	3
1	12	22

Centre layer

18	25	2
4	19	21
14	11	8

Bottom layer

15	27	13
24	5	16
20	7	9

The colours of the faces of the above cube are:
1 Looking down on the cube – Yellow.
2 Looking from beneath the cube – Violet.
3 The remaining faces are as shown below:

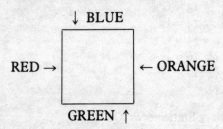

↓ BLUE

RED → ← ORANGE

GREEN ↑

A93 People's Pets Q43

George Anderson lives in Chestnut Crescent and he has a pet budgie called Percy. The full solution is as follows:

1. Tom Williams owns the fish called Fred and lives in Maple Grove.

2. John Thompson owns the dog called Benson and lives in Cedar Road.

3. Bill Smith owns the rabbit called Rodney and lives in Pine Avenue.

4. George Anderson owns the budgie called Percy and lives in Chestnut Crescent.

5. Harry Hudson owns the cat called Spike and lives in Willow Street.

```
I C E
D G A
H B F
```

A95   Connection   Q60

2. If the squares are numbered 1 to 9 as if reading conventionally, the following changes occur:

Square 1 – contents move to square 3.
Square 2 – they move to square 1.
Square 3 – they move to square 2.
Square 4 – they move to square 5.
Square 5 – they move to square 6.
Square 6 – they move to square 4.
Squares 7, 8 and 9 – the two circles within each square move to the two corners of the square which did not originally contain a circle.

A96   Whodunnit?   Q75

Lady Logic killed her husband with the hammer.

A97   Odd Block Out   Q77

Number 3 is the odd one out as all of the others are different views of the same block.

A98   Coin Puzzle   Q91

Form a square with three coins on each side, then place another coin on top of each corner coin.

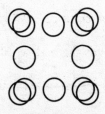

F	O	D	N
G	B	I	C
H	J	A	K
E	M	P	L

A100   Odd Block Out   Q111
Number 8 is the odd one out as all of the others are different views of the same block.

A101   Odd One Out   Q120
A.

A102   Odd One Out   Q129
B.

A103   Logic Cube   Q136

TOP LAYER: BACK

K	Y	A
Q	T	D
J	V	N

FRONT

MIDDLE LAYER: BACK

@	S	G
P	B	W
C	H	U

FRONT

BOTTOM LAYER: BACK

X	E	O
M	F	I
R	Z	L

FRONT

A104 Flipover Q6

The letters were flipped over the numbers shown in brackets in the following direction:

(1) – vertically;
(2) – horizontally;
(3) – horizontally;
(4) – vertically.

A105 Done What? Q19

Dave did it. If only one person is telling the truth and Charlie didn't do it, then it must be Charlie who is telling the truth as he said that he didn't do it. Therefore all of the other statements must be false. Dave said that Bill did it which isn't true, Bill said that Arthur did it which isn't true and Arthur said that Eddie did it which also isn't true. The only person remaining who could have done it is Dave.

A106 Flipover Q35

The letters were flipped over the numbers shown in brackets in the following order and direction:

(2) – vertically;
(1) – horizontally;
(2) – vertically;
(3) – horizontally;
(4) – vertically;
(3) – horizontally.

A107 Logicalympics – 100 Metres Q49

Race	1st	2nd	3rd	4th	5th
1	A	B	C	D	E
2	D	E	A	B	C
3	B	C	D	E	A
4	E	A	B	C	D
5	C	D	E	A	B

A108 Piano Lessons Q66

	MORNING		AFTERNOON	
	NAME	GRADE	NAME	GRADE
MONDAY	BRIAN	ONE	JOHN	THREE
TUESDAY	SUSAN	TWO	BRIAN	ONE
WEDNESDAY	JILL	FIVE	LUCY	FOUR
THURSDAY	TOMMY	ONE	JULIE	THREE
FRIDAY	LUCY	FOUR	SUSAN	TWO

A109 Sweet Tooth Q78
Tracey – toffee;

Alan – chocolate-covered mints;

James – plain mints;

Robert – mint-flavoured toffee;

Neil – chocolate.

A110 Odd One Out Q100
Number 8. All of the others remain the same if flipped over about
the vertical, horizontal or any of the two main diagonal axes.

A111 What Next? Q113
Six

Three

Five

There is one word between the two 'ones', two words between the
two 'twos', three words between the two 'threes', etc.

A112 Mix Up 16 Q126

1	2	3	4	5	6	7	8	9	10	11	12	13	14	15	16
2	6	9	13	1	5	10	14	8	4	15	11	7	3	16	12
3	9	12	2	14	8	5	15	11	1	4	10	6	16	13	7
4	13	2	15	10	7	12	5	6	11	8	9	16	1	14	3
5	1	14	10	6	2	13	9	3	7	12	16	4	8	11	15
6	5	8	7	2	1	4	3	14	13	16	15	10	9	12	11
7	10	5	12	13	4	15	2	1	16	3	14	11	6	9	8
8	14	15	5	9	3	2	12	16	6	7	13	1	11	10	4
9	8	11	6	3	14	1	16	15	2	13	4	5	12	7	10
10	4	1	11	7	13	16	6	2	12	9	3	15	5	8	14
11	15	4	8	12	16	3	7	13	9	6	2	14	10	5	1
12	11	10	9	16	15	14	13	4	3	2	1	8	7	6	5
13	7	6	16	4	10	11	1	5	15	14	8	12	2	3	9
14	3	16	1	8	9	6	11	12	5	10	7	2	15	4	13
15	16	13	14	11	12	9	10	7	8	5	6	3	4	1	2
16	12	7	3	15	11	8	4	10	14	1	5	9	13	2	6

A113 Logic Cube Q130

TOP LAYER: BACK

Z	G	D
U	W	O
A	J	N

FRONT

MIDDLE LAYER: BACK

P	V	C
J	K	O
F	X	B

FRONT

BOTTOM LAYER: BACK

R	Y	H
L	E	@
M	S	I

FRONT

A114 Temple Teaser Q137

The order of the statues, from right to left, is as follows: Moirai, Ate, Nike, Rhea, Nemesis, Hebe, Pleiades, Iris, Chloris, Hygiea, Opis, Terpsichore, Amphitrite, Artemis, Eos, Tyche, Danae, Hestia, Selene, Hera, Athene, Persephone, Irene, Aphrodite, Hecate, Demeter.

A115 Letter Boxes Q9

D	E	F	H	I	J	C	G	B	A
F	C	G	A	J	E	H	D	I	B
E	B	A	I	C	D	G	J	H	F
B	D	H	C	E	G	I	A	F	J
I	J	E	G	B	H	F	C	A	D
A	G	C	B	D	I	E	F	J	H
C	H	B	J	G	F	A	I	D	E
J	F	I	E	H	A	D	B	C	G
G	I	D	F	A	B	J	H	E	C
H	A	J	D	F	C	B	E	G	I

203

A116 Connection Q37

5. There are four stages in the connection between the squares.

1. All three columns of squares are overlapped and combined to form the column on the left of the connecting square.

2. The resulting figure in the top square of the left-hand column is then duplicated into the bottom square of the centre column and the centre square of the right-hand column.

3. The resulting figure in the centre square of the left-hand column is then duplicated into the top square of the centre column and the bottom square of the right-hand column.

4. The resulting figure in the bottom square of the left-hand column is then duplicated into the centre square of the centre column and the top square of the right-hand column.

A117 Uncle Christmas Q50

Uncle George will get the scarf for Christmas. (Uncle Raymond will get the gloves, Uncle Victor the hat and Uncle John the tie.)

A118 Logic Box Q68

```
H B E
D C G
I A F
```

A119 Boxed Q81

	Left			Right
Box colour:	Red	Yellow	Green	Blue
Glove colour:	Green	Blue	Red	Yellow
Scarf colour:	Blue	Red	Yellow	Green

A120 Clockwork Links Q102

The letters around the numbers given in brackets were rotated in the following order and direction:

(1) – 90° clockwise;
(2) – 90° clockwise;
(4) – 180°;
(3) – 180°;
(4) – 90° clockwise;
(2) – 180°;
(1) – 90° anticlockwise;
(3) – 90° anticlockwise.

A121 Logic Box Q112

O	C	N	B
P	H	A	I
D	G	M	E
J	L	F	K

A122 Advanced Academics Q146

ALWIN	ANSON	ABNER	ANTON	ALWYN
ABDUL	ATHOL	ALVES	ABRAM	ALBAN
AUBYN	AIRAY	ARIEL	ALBAT	AMAND
ALGIE	ANGUS	AARON	ALLAN	ARCHY
ANDRE	ALROY	ASKEW	AUREL	ALRED

A123 Whodunnit? Q140

The butler killed Lady Logic in the kitchen using the knife.

A124 What Next? Q11

The next most appropriate square is C.

Each square is divided into four smaller squares. All four of which contain two changes each time the sequence progresses.

1. TOP LEFT-HAND SQUARE: The dot moves from corner to corner of the square in an anticlockwise direction and the 'T' lines rotate 45° in a clockwise direction.

2. TOP RIGHT-HAND SQUARE: The dot moves from corner to corner of the square in a clockwise direction and the straight line rotates 45° in an anticlockwise direction.

3. BOTTOM LEFT-HAND SQUARE: The dot moves from corner to corner of the square in an anticlockwise direction and the straight line rotates 45° in a clockwise direction.

4. BOTTOM RIGHT-HAND SQUARE: The dot moves from corner to corner of the square in a clockwise direction and the 'T' lines rotate 45° in an anticlockwise direction.

A125 The History of Invention Q17

Invention	Year
Gunpowder	1320
The telescope	1607
Pianoforte	1710
The mercury thermometer	1721
The spinning jenny	1763
The steam engine	1764
The hot air balloon	1783
The miner's safety lamp	1815
The sewing machine	1841
Steel	1856
Dynamite	1868
The telephone	1876
The phonograph	1877
The wireless	1898
The tank	1899
Radar	1935
The jet engine	1939
Polyester	1941

A126 Done What? Q31
Charlie did it.

A127 All the Twos Q42
1. Eric and Alex.
2. Frank and Doug.
The results of the two races are as follows:

Race	One	Two
1st	Eric	Colin
2nd	Alex	Brad
3rd	Colin	Eric
4th	Brad	Alex
5th	Frank	Frank
6th	Doug	Doug

A128 Done What? Q59
Harry did it.

A129 Odd One Out Q79
C.

A130 Grid Fill Q94
The words can also be fitted into the grid in a mirror image (diagonally) of the solution shown below.

A131   Say Cheese   Q105
From left to right: Cheddar, Edam, Tilsiter, Pecorino, Port Salut, Parmesan, Jarlsberg, Roquefort, Cheshire, Brickbat, Swiss, Cotswold, Lymeswold, Camembert, Gorgonzola, Wensleydale, Gouda, Brie, Gruyère, Gloucester, Cottage, Gambozola, Stilton, Mycella, Boursin, Westminster Blue.

A132   Clockwork Links   Q121
The letters around the numbers given in brackets were rotated in the following order and direction:

(1) – 90° clockwise;
(2) – 90° anticlockwise;
(4) – 180°;
(2) – 90° clockwise;
(4) – 180°;
(3) – 90° clockwise;
(1) – 180°;
(3) – 90° anticlockwise.

A133   Blocked   Q132
Blocks rotated clockwise = A3, A4, B2, B5, C2, C3, C4, C5, D1, D5, E3, E4, E5;
Blocks rotated anticlockwise = A1, A2, A5, B1, B3, B4, C1, D2, D3, D4, E1, E2.

A134   Blocked   Q12
Blocks rotated anticlockwise = A2, B1, B2, Ĉ3, C4, D3, D5;
Blocks rotated clockwise = A4, B5, D1, D3, E1, E4.

A135   Safecracker   Q61
4 2 1 3 is the correct combination.

A136   Somewhere   Q73
Do you live here? If you are in village A the answer will be yes. If you are in village B the answer will be no. It does not matter if the resident is actually from the village or not, the answer would still be the same.

A137   Odd Block Out   Q46
Number 6 is the odd block out. All the others are different views of
the same block.

A138   Connection   Q104
5. Each of the 25 small squares contain a cross, or, a circle. In the
connecting square, all of the crosses of the original square have
been deleted, as have the circles which were in the centre of a
diagonal, vertical, or horizontal line of three squares, with the two
other squares in the line containing a cross.

A139   Wordsquare   Q14

A140   Clockwork   Q53
The letters around the numbers given in brackets were rotated in
the following order and direction:

(2) – 90° anticlockwise;
(4) – 180°;
(3) – 90° clockwise;
(1) – 180°;
(2) – 90° clockwise;
(3) – 180°;
(4) – 90° anticlockwise.

The first two rotations could be the other way round, i.e. (4) – 180°
and then (2) – 90° anticlockwise, as there is no further effect on
either until the letters around the number (3) are rotated.

A141   Letter Boxes   Q108

```
B   E   D   A   I   F   H   C   J   G
C   I   E   D   G   A   J   F   H   B
G   C   J   F   H   D   I   A   B   E
I   H   B   C   A   J   E   G   D   F
A   J   I   E   B   C   G   D   F   H
E   A   F   J   D   B   C   H   G   I
D   B   A   G   C   H   F   E   I   J
J   F   H   B   E   G   D   I   C   A
H   G   C   I   F   E   B   J   A   D
F   D   G   H   J   I   A   B   E   C
```

A142   Letter Boxes   Q83

```
A   B   D   F   C   G   E   I   J   H
F   H   J   D   E   A   I   G   C   B
H   I   B   G   J   E   C   F   D   A
E   A   C   I   G   F   D   B   H   J
J   F   E   C   D   B   A   H   G   I
D   G   F   B   A   J   H   C   I   E
C   D   A   J   I   H   F   E   B   G
B   J   I   E   H   D   G   A   F   C
I   E   G   H   B   C   J   D   A   F
G   C   H   A   F   I   B   J   E   D
```

A143   Letter Boxes   Q32

```
G   I   C   F   A   D   B   J   H   E
E   C   B   A   I   F   J   D   H   G   H
C   G   A   H   F   E   D   I   J   B
D   E   F   G   H   J   A   B   C   I
J   H   I   D   G   B   E   C   A   F
A   D   H   B   J   G   F   E   I   C
F   J   G   E   D   C   I   H   B   A
H   F   D   C   B   I   G   A   E   J
I   B   E   J   C   A   H   G   F   D
B   A   J   I   E   H   C   F   D   G
```

A144   Where Do They Live?   Q21
1 – Brown;
2 – Johnson;
3 – Anderson;
4 – Bainbridge;
5 – Charlton.

A145   Blocked   Q48
Blocks rotated clockwise = A1, B5, C2, D4, E1;
Blocks rotated anticlockwise = A4, B3, C3, D2, E5;
Blocks rotated 180° = A3, B1, C4, D5, E2.

A146   Connection   Q16
4. (The square has been flipped over about the horizontal axis.)

A147   Sequence   Q156
Between the numbers six and three. The numbers are in alphabetical order.

A)   20.   The sequence is the position of the letter in the alphabet of the first letter in the numbers 1 to 12 when given in full, *e.g.*: *ONE O* = 15.

B)   81.   The sequence comprises whole numbers beginning with a vowel.

C)   32.   The sequence comprises whole numbers containing the letter O.

D)   2.   The sequence is as follows; there is one number between the two 1's, two numbers between the two 2's, three numbers between the two 3's and four numbers between the two 4's.

E)   205. $1 + 1 \times 2 + 3 \times 4 + 5 \times 6 + 7$

F)   70.   Sum of digits in all previous numbers in the sequence.

G)   307.   Difference divided by three and added to last number.

H)   4895.   Each number is multiplied by its rank in the sequence, and the next number is subtracted. $9 \times 1 - 2 = 7 \times 3 - 4 = 17 \times 5 - 6 = 79 \times 7 - 8 = 545 \times 9 - 10 = 4895$.

I)   21.   They all begin with the letter T.

J)   52.   The numbers are the totals of the letters in the words ONE, TWO, THREE, FOUR, FIVE and SIX, when A = 1, B = 2, C = 3 etc.

A149   Word Square Links   Q232

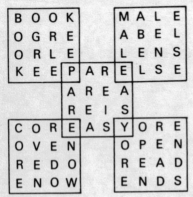

A150 One-word Q162

1 Emaciated; 2 Direction; 3 Tailoring; 4 Personate;
5 Uncertain; 6 Variously; 7 Eradicate; 8 Organised;
9 Cessation; 10 Calibrate; 11 Insomniac; 12 Incognito;
13 Medicinal; 14 Schematic; 15 Astringed; 16 Lamenting;
17 Diligence; 18 Continual

A151 Three Too Many Q248

B	E	N	E	A	T	H
A		A			A	
U	N	K	E	M	P	T
L		E		A		I
K	I	D	D	I	N	G
	L			Z		H
C	L	E	M	E	N	T

A152 Ending Q197
UMP

A153 Laser Q177
A7 = X; D4 = X; D5 = X; E10 = X; C3 = Y; F4 = Y; H8 = Y; J8 = Y; E8 = Z; I6 = Z

A154 Qwerty Q206
Proprietory and Rupturewort.

213

A155 Diagonal Square Q241

38	6	16	33	43	11	28
46	14	24	41	2	19	29
5	15	32	49	10	27	37
13	23	40	1	18	35	45
21	31	48	9	26	36	4
22	39	7	17	34	44	12
30	47	8	25	42	3	20

A156 Crossbits 3 Q253

```
P A S S E N G E R   R O A S T
E   M       O   E   E       R
N E E D L E R   L A T A K I A
N   L   E   S E E   R   E   C
Y E L L O W Y   A   E L D E R
P       A     S E A   G     I
I N T E S T A T E   D R E A M
N   M   T   A   B   O     O N
C L O U D   E M U L A T I O N
H   P   I M P     U         I
I L E U S     I   G E S T A P O
N   R   T   C U E   E   M   U
G R A N U L E   N E W N E S S
  A   R   D   I       N     L
T H U M B   E X C I T E D L Y
```

```
U S U R I O U S   T I P   K
  E   E   C   C   R   E P I C
A G E D   T E R M I T E   L
  M   I   E   E   T   P I N E
D E P A R T   E   I R E     S
  N   E   O D I C   R E A P
S T A T E   U   A   T     R
T   E   D A T A B L E   N   I
I   O   M   A   L E A S T
G O N E   N E O N   S   H
M   S K I   R   G E N D E R
A U N T   O   D E   O   A
  R   E N T R A I N   S A V E
O G L E   I   I   E   E   E
  E   M A C   N A T U R I S T
```

A157 What Next? Q154

O It is the second letter in MONDAY. The sequence is the second letter of each day of the week in reverse, starting at Sunday.

A158 Mini Crossnumber Q186

```
1 5 4
2 1 6
1 2 5
```

A159 Letter Grid – Biblical Characters Q218

Asa, Eve, Job, Lot, Abel, Adam, Ahab, Boaz, Cain, Esau, Jude, Leah, Levi, Mark, Moab, Paul, Ruth, Saul, Caleb, Enoch, Hiram, Hosea, Joash, Linus, Satan, Sihon, Silas, Titus, Uriel, Zadok, Andrew, Darius, Dorcas, Elijah, Elisha, Esther, Isaiah, Jairus, Miriam, Naboth, Rachel, Reuben, Samuel, Yahweh, Malachi, Meshach, Timothy, Zebulon, Gamaliel, Philemon, Zedekiah, Abimelech, Zacchaeus, Zephaniah, Bartimaeus, Belshazzar, Holofernes, Methuselah, Theophilus, Bartholomew, Jehoshaphat, Melchizedek, Sennacherib, Mary Magdalene, Pontius Pilate, John the Baptist, Nebuchadnezzar.

This reveals the alphabetical sequence ABCDEFGHIJKLMNOPQRSTUVWXYZ.

A160 Magic Letter Square Q244
K − Z = 1 to 16 respectively.

K	N	X	Y	U	T	R	O
W	Z	L	M	Q	P	V	S
R	O	U	T	X	Y	K	N
V	S	Q	P	L	M	W	Z
P	V	S	Q	Z	L	M	W
Y	K	N	X	O	U	T	R
M	W	Z	L	S	Q	P	V
T	R	O	U	N	X	Y	K

A161 Triplegram Q167
A Perviously; B Previously; C Viperously.

A162 Which Word? Q198
POT All of the other words can be 'doubled' to form another word:
BYEBYE, CANCAN, GEEGEE etc.

A163 Inner Word Square Q231
```
C A T C H
A W A R E
T A P E R
C R E D O
H E R O N
```

216

O	P	T		A	S	P		E	B	B
F		A	R	C		R	O	C		Y
F	I	X		E	G	O		U	R	E
	N			E			E			
S	K	I		E	L	L		O	D	E
P		M	A	Y		U	R	N		R
Y	A	P		E	L	M		E	K	E
	I			U			O			
E	R	A		A	G	E		A	P	E
S		N	I	P		F	A	D		O
S	U	E		T	A	T		D	O	N

A165   Missing Letters   Q152

U and X. The 1st, 3rd, 5th, 7th and 9th letters are the vowels in reverse order. If you then number the letters of the alphabet A–Z, 1–26 respectively, and again 27–52 respectively, the letter between each of the vowels is the letter equal to their total in the previously numbered alphabet.

U	K	O	X	I	N	E	F	A
22	37	15	24	9	14	5	6	1

A166   Bullseye   Q192

Player 3   From the information given, all you can work out is if the scores were odd or even. As only player 3 could have scored an odd score of 451 to finish on a bullseye, the solution is player 3.

A167   Power Puzzle   Q222

A = 1; B = 0; C = 3; D = 5; E = 7; F = 4; G = 2

A168   A Good Year   Q180

1	7	1	1	8	9
1	1	9	4	1	1
1	4	2	6	2	4
2	5	1	8	7	3
1	2	3	2	2	3

A169   Smile Please   Q172
Alroy

A170   Code One   Q229
The message reads:
'Each letter in this message has been replaced by the triangular number corresponding to its position in the alphabet.'

A = 1	J = 55	S = 190
B = 3	K = 66	T = 210
C = 6	L = 78	U = 231
D = 10	M = 91	V = 253
E = 15	N = 105	W = 276
F = 21	O = 120	X = 300
G = 28	P = 136	Y = 325
H = 36	Q = 153	Z = 351
I = 45	R = 171	

Triangular numbers are formed by adding up the series $1 + 2 + 3 + 4 + 5 + 6 \ldots \ldots$

A171   Number Boxes   Q158
B.   Both A and C add up when read left to right and counting the right-hand column first.
e.g. 583 + 146 = 729
715 + 248 = 963

0 = L; 1 = E; 2 = O; 3 = C; 4 = A; 5 = S; 6 = T; 7 = I;
8 = N

T		A	S	S	A	I	L	A	N	T		T	I	C
A	L	T	O		L		I		O		O			L
C		O	S	E	C		O	C	T	E	T	T	E	
T	I	N	E	A		A		L		E		A		A
		A		L	A	S	S	I	E		C	L	A	N
A	L	L	O	T	T	E	E		N	I	L			
	I		S		T		C		T		I	N	T	O
	N		C	O	A	S	T	L	I	N	E		E	
S	O	L	I		I		I		T		N		E	
		N	O	N		O	I	L	S	T	O	N	E	
L	I	N	E		T	I	N	S	E	L		L		
A		I		N		N		L		I	L	E	A	L
T	O	E	N	A	I	L		E	A	T		A		A
E		C		N		E			L		O	T	I	C
N	E	E		A	N	T	I	C	L	I	N	E		E

A173   Letter Grid – Rivers   Q214

Allan, Avoca, Bann, Cher, Chindwin, Clarence, Colorado, Dela-
ware, Dniester, Dunajec, Eden, Gatineau, Guadiana, Gumti,
Hamble, Irtish, Kennebec, Kootenay, Loire, Lugendi, Niemen,
Orange, Porali, Putumayo, Ribble, Swan, Test, Ucayali, Wanga-
nui, Weser, Winnipeg, Yarrow, Yuruari.
The revealed river is the Mississippi.

A174   Magic Square   Q237

17	29	11	23
7	27	13	33
21	9	31	19
35	15	25	5

A175 Logic Box Q170

G	E	B
C	A	I
H	D	F

A176 Cubes Q147
3 and 5.

A177 Crossbits 2 Q251

```
.  A  .  S  .  R  .  H  E  A  D  R  E  S  T
P  R  O  T  R  U  D  E  .  D  .  O  .  .  H
.  G  .  E  .  C  .  A  D  D  U  C  T  .  R
H  U  L  L  .  T  O  P  I  .  N  .  E  V  E
.  M  .  L  .  I  .  .  S  E  P  I  A  .  A
S  E  N  A  T  O  R  .  A  .  A  .  S  I  T
.  N  .  R  .  N  .  A  R  R  I  V  E  .  E
A  T  E  .  A  .  E  L  M  .  D  .  T  E  N
L  .  N  E  T  T  L  E  .  .  S  A  .  M  .
L  O  T  .  T  .  D  .  M  I  S  C  O  P  Y
O  .  I  N  U  R  E  .  .  .  C  .  L  .  .
C  A  R  .  N  .  S  A  L  T  .  U  P  O  N
A  .  E  V  E  N  T  S  .  E  .  S  .  Y  .
T  .  .  I  .  O  .  H  A  R  D  E  N  E  R
E  X  P  E  R  T  L  Y  .  Y  .  D  .  R  .
```

```
P R E S S   S T U D     S C A L D
  O   A       O   A   C   L   O
A B O V E   P A R C H   A M P
  L   E   A     K   O   T   E
L E A D E N L Y     O V E R
O   N   G       S O L O   O
O V E N   L E A P     I O T A
S   L A D E N   E D U C T   B
E W E R     O N C E   E T C H
  H   K N O W   E       E   O
  Y O Y O     D O D D E R E R
S   C   B   L     Y   A   V
T I C   B L E E D   I S L E T
E   U   L   S   E     E   N
M O R S E   S A N D G L A S S
```

A179 Power Property Q224

$A = 5$; $B = 8$; $C = 6$; $D = 2$; $E = 4$; $F = 9$; $G = 1$; $H = 7$;
$I = 3$

$$183,184 = 428^2$$
$$528,529 = 727^2$$
$$715,716 = 846^2$$

These are the only numbers with six figures which are a square whose digits form two consecutive numbers.

A180 Jigsum Q187

4	+	6	×	5	/	2	+	5	/	3
+	–	+	■	+	■	×	■	×	×	+
9	/	3	×	8	+	6	–	5	–	5
+	■	+	×	–	■	×	–	×	■	+
4	/	2	×	9	×	2	–	1	–	5
–	■	+	■	×	+	+	■	×	■	+
7	+	7	+	8	×	3	/	2	+	7
+	■	–	×	+	■	+	×	/	■	/
3	×	3	–	3	×	5	–	5	×	2
–	–	+	■	–	■	+	■	×	/	×
3	×	5	–	5	–	8	×	5	×	6

A181 Letter Grid – Hats Q210

Balaclava, bearskin, beret, boater, bonnet, bowler, busby, cap, coronet, deerstalker, derby, fez, gibus, glengarry, homburg, kepi, mitre, panama, peaked, shako, sombrero, stetson, tile, titfer, top, trilby.

The revealed song line is 'Wherever I lay my hat, that's my home.'

A182 Block Total Q179

B = 8; L = 7; O = 5; C = 9; K = 4

A183 Grid Zero Q243

A	B	D	E	D	C	F	C
E	C	D	B	C	F	A	D
D	E	B	A	F	C	C	D
C	F	C	D	B	A	D	E
C	C	A	F	E	D	D	B
F	D	E	C	A	D	B	C
B	D	F	D	C	E	C	A
D	A	C	C	D	B	E	F

222

A184 Letter Grid – Professions Q211

Apiarist, artist, baker, ballerina, bellboy, bosun, bursar, chauffeur, costumier, editor, enameller, envoy, farmer, fireman, florist, hotelier, indexer, navvy, nurse, painter, pantler, publisher, puppeteer, rabbi, raftsman, roundsman, rugmaker, shearer, squire, stainer, tiler, tinker, typist, usher, vocalist.

The revealed occupation is lamplighter.

A185 Crossbits 1 Q250

P	O	R	T	I	O	N		C		T	O	U	C	H
	U		I			E	R	R	O	R		S		E
S	T	A	L	E		A		O		O		E		A
	G		E		S	T	O	P		T	I	D	A	L
G	R	A	S	S		N			A		N		N	
				A	E	R	O	B	I	C		I		
A	W	E	L	E	S	S			O		A	B	L	E
S		O		E	S	T	E	R			O		W	
K	I	N	D		I			N	A	R	R	A	T	E
	T		E	N	T	H	R	A	L			U		
	E		A		Y			R		G	O	R	G	E
S	M	A	L	L		E	A	C	H		C		B	
E		U		O		D		H		E	T	H	O	S
A		N		L	E	D	G	E			A		A	
T	O	T	A	L		Y		D	E	F	L	A	T	E

A186 Two Halves Q157

228 The letters of the alphabet have been numbered 1 to 26 respectively. Therefore,

$F + R + O + M + A + T + O + M = 202$ and $F + R + O + M + N + T + O + Z = 228$.

A187 High Scorer Q189

99 (25 + 18 + 17 + 20 + 19)

A188 Power Puzzle Q221

A = 4; B = 3; C = 8; D = 5; E = 7; F = 9; G = 0.

A189 Paint Puzzle Q174

1 Buff; 2 Gamboge; 3 Plain yellow; 4 Gilt; 5 Sulphur;
6 Aureate; 7 Xanthic; 8 Primrose; 9 Fallow; 10 Topaz;
11 Cream; 12 Saffron; 13 Amber; 14 Gold; 15 Guilded;
16 Lemon

A190 Letter Grid – Capitals Q207

Agana, Amman, Amsterdam, Andorra, Belgrade, Berne,
Budapest, Bujumbura, Cairo, Damascus, Doha, Islamabad, Jeru-
salem, Luanda, Madrid, Male, Maputo, Mogadishu, Nukualofa,
Ottawa, Pyongyang, Rabat, Rangoon, Reykjavik, Saigon, Salis-
bury, Seoul, Sofia, Stockholm, Vienna, Vientiane.
The revealed capital is Copenhagen.

A191 Magic Square Tiles Q239

1	9	5	1	6	8	3	4	8
6	2	7	9	2	4	5	9	1
8	4	3	5	7	3	7	2	6
5	7	3	6	2	7	5	9	4
1	6	8	8	4	3	7	2	6
9	2	4	1	9	5	3	4	8
3	4	8	9	2	4	8	4	3
5	9	1	5	7	3	1	9	5
7	2	6	1	6	8	6	2	7

A192 Magic Cube Q245

A

61	09	05	49
17	37	41	29
33	21	25	45
13	57	53	01

B

14	34	18	62
58	22	38	10
54	26	42	06
02	46	30	50

C

03	55	59	15
47	27	23	35
31	43	39	19
51	07	11	63

D

52	32	48	04
08	44	28	56
12	40	24	60
64	20	36	16

A193 0 to 12 in Nine Q188

4	×	7	+	9	= 37
×	×	+	×	×	
6	−	1	×	3	= 15
+	+	×	+	−	
2	×	5	×	8	= 80

= 11   = 26   = 40   = 19   = 12

A194 Safe and Sound Q182

Tower number 1 = 6
,,   ,,   2 = 1
,,   ,,   3 = 4
,,   ,,   4 = 2
,,   ,,   5 = 5
,,   ,,   6 = 3

A195 Age Old Question Q151
Edward.

A196 Letter Grid – Composers Q216
Arne, Bax, Beethoven, Bellini, Benedict, Berlin, Byrd, Cesti, Couperin, Cui, Debussy, Elgar, Ives, Kern, Kreisler, Mahler, Monteverdi, Mozart, Mussorgsky, Offenbach, Scarlatti, Searle, Sibelius, Sousa, Spontini, Stravinsky, Zarenski.
The revealed name is Lloyd-Webber.

A197 Cryptogram Limerick Q227

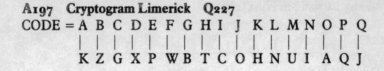

CODE = A B C D E F G H I J K L M N O P Q
       | | | | | | | | | | | | | | | | |
       K Z G X P W B T C O H N U I A Q J

       R S T U V W X Y Z
       | | | | | | | | |
       S D M R E Y F L V

The limerick reads:

THERE'S A WONDERFUL FAMILY CALLED STEIN,
THERE'S GERT AND THERE'S EPP AND THERE'S EIN;
GERT'S POEMS ARE BUNK,
EPP'S STATUES ARE JUNK,
AND NO ONE CAN UNDERSTAND EIN.

(Gertrude Stein, Jacob Epstein, Albert Einstein.)

A198 All in Line Q196
AIL (All In Line)

A199 Triplegram Q169
A Discounter; B Introduces; C Reductions.

A200 Squares in Square Q238

02	16	15	05
13	07	08	10
09	11	12	06
14	04	03	17

A201 ABC Crossword Q249
Across
a Give; d Eastern; g Avon; h Store; i Cleaver; k Debit; l Untwist; n Nightwatchman; s Misty; q Agitate; t Plumage; u Short; v Noah; w Clement; x Door

Down
a Gathering; b Varnish; c Eve; d Encouragement; e Sceptic; f Envoi; j Rot; m Scatterer; o Teacake; p Heigh Ho; q Alp; r Inure; u Sad

A202 Letter Boxes Q148

1 O (October)
  N (November)
  D (December)

The box contains the initial letters of the 12 months of the year.

2 S (Scorpio)
  T (Taurus)
  V (Virgo)

The box contains the initial letters of the signs of the zodiac in alphabetical order.

A203 Letter Grid – Dances Q212

Arabesque, bebop, beguine, bolero, bossa nova, boston, charleston, fandango, hornpipe, jig, jive, juba, kolo, mambo, pooka-pooka, rondo, saltarello, saraband, shimmy, strathspey, tambourine, tarantella, tripudiary, valeta.

The revealed dance is the Paul Jones.

A204 Cryptogram Quotation Q225

CODE = A B C D E F G H I J K L M N O P Q
       | | | | | | | | | | | | | | | | |
       M A Z Y H T E I R C S K Q W D J U

       R S T U V W X Y Z
       | | | | | | | | |
       P F L V G X N B O

Quotation reads:

    'THE TIME HAS COME,' THE WALRUS SAID,
      'TO TALK OF MANY THINGS;
  OF SHOES—AND SHIPS—AND SEALING WAX—
      OF CABBAGES—AND KINGS—
    AND WHY THE SEA IS BOILING HOT—
    AND WHETHER PIGS HAVE WINGS.'

        (Lewis Carroll.)

A205 One-word Q161

1 Veritable; 2 Sectional; 3 Medicated; 4 Versatile;
5 Topically; 6 Reduction; 7 Simmering; 8 Laudation;
9 Stationed; 10 Tangerine; 11 Omissible; 12 Signatory;
13 Assurance; 14 Carnalise; 15 Centurion; 16 Ancestral;
17 Operating; 18 Nostalgia.

A206 Crossnumber Q193

Across

1 5184; 4 6561; 7 125; 9 757; 10 31; 11 216; 12 3721;
14 1521; 15 8649; 16 6859; 19 2116; 22 7744; 24 937; 25 17;
26 701; 27 163; 28 3969; 29 6241

Down

2 1225; 3 4761; 4 653; 5 5776; 6 11; 7 12167; 8 512;
10 324; 13 19683; 17 877; 18 5476; 19 2916; 20 131; 21 1764;
23 409; 25 13

A207 Crossword Q247

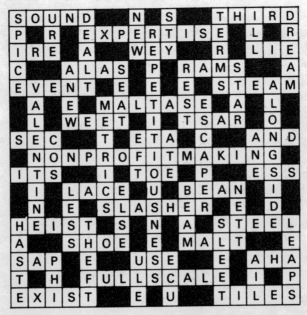

A208 All the Fours Q240

144	8	12	136	20	124
28	116	36	40	104	120
52	80	88	84	68	72
96	56	64	60	92	76
100	44	112	108	32	48
24	140	132	16	128	4

A209 The Round Table Q175
Galahad.

A210 Letter Grid – Vehicles Q208
Ambulance, bandwagon, bubblecar, bulldozer, bus, cablecar, cacolet, chaise, chariot, clarence, coach, dennet, drosky, duck, hansom cab, landaulet, quadriga, rickshaw, roadster, scooter, sedan, surrey, tank, tender, train, tricycle, troika, van.
This reveals perambulator (pram).

A211 Double Quote Q228
'Give us the tools, and we will finish the job.'
Sir Winston Leonard Spencer Churchill (30/11/1874–24/1/1965)
(Broadcast address, 9 Feb 1941).

'What is our task? To make Britain a fit country for heroes to live in.'
David Lloyd George, 1st Earl (17/1/1863–26/3/1945)
(Speech, Wolverhampton, 24 Nov 1918)

Both were at one time British Prime Ministers.

A212 Prime Crossnumber Q190
Across
a 431; d 373; e 263; g 397; h 727; k 251; l 479; m 991; n 193; p 317; q 823; r 197
Down
a 433; b 379; c 137; e 229; f 659; g 311; h 743; i 271; j 797; n 181; o 929; p 337

A213 Letter Value Q181

A	B	C	D	E	F	G	H	I	J	K	L	M	N	O	P	Q	R	S
8	25	2	12	20	4	14	3	7	13	1	19	5	21	24	15	6	18	23

T	U	V	W	X	Y	Z
11	16	9	26	17	22	10

A214 Words Q150

1 UNDERGONE. The vowels have been given the following
values: A = 1; E = 2; I = 3; O = 4; U = 5

COMPATIBLE = 10   CURIE = 10

AUDIENCE = 13   UNDERGONE = 13

2 311.   Position in alphabet multiplied by position in word for
each letter gives the total value for each word when added
together.

eg. SOUND = $(19 \times 1) + (15 \times 2) + (21 \times 3) + (14 \times 4) + (4 \times 5)$
= 188

A215 Power Puzzle Q219

A = 6; B = 1; C = 5; D = 8; E = 2; F = 4; G = 9; H = 3;
I = 7

$6578 = 1^4 + 2^4 + 9^4 = 3^4 + 7^4 + 8^4$

A216 One-word Q163

1 Intoxicate; 2 Straighten; 3 Gloominess; 4 Coagulated;
5 Engrasping; 6 Instrument; 7 Emphatical; 8 Dictionary;
9 Supersonic; 10 Marginally

A217 Code Clue Q230

Even though one of the letters has been placed in a grid, it does not
mean that it is in the correct place, or, that the grid is of any use in
solving the puzzle. The grid was no more than a distraction. If you
write down the sentences backwards, the following appears:

When setting crossword clues, a question mark is used when the puzzle setter is feeling benevolent and wishes to draw attention to a double meaning. In effect, it warns that the answer, while relating well to one half of the clue, only responds to the other half in a punning or cryptic way.

A218   Letter Blocks   Q201
1 Absent; 2 Blazon; 3 Dahlia; 4 Eureka; 5 Frugal; 6 Hyaena;
7 Loofah; 8 Ocelot; 9 Podium; 10 Rhumba; 11 Tickle;
12 Woeful

A219   Clockwork   Q176
Starting with diagram A, move 2–90° clockwise,
3–180°
4–180°
1–90° clockwise
3–180°
2–90° anticlockwise
4–90° anticlockwise

A220   Word Cube   Q236

TOP		
A	S	A
S	E	C
A	C	E

CENTRE		
N	E	W
E	R	A
W	A	Y

BOTTOM		
T	E	E
E	A	R
E	R	E

The 18 words formed are:
ACE; ARE; ANT; AWE; CAR; EAR; EAT; ERA; ERE
EYE; NEW; SEC; SEE; TAE; TEE; WAY; WEN; YAW

A221   Pentagon   Q184
A = 14; B = 1; C = 9; D = 8; E = 5; F = 11; G = 13;
H = 7; I = 4; J = 3; K = 15; L = 6; M = 2; N = 12;
O = 10

A222 Division Q160

INCOMPREHENSIBLE

IRRESPONSIBILITY

MISUNDERSTANDING

MISPRONUNCIATION

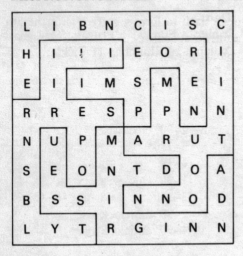

A223 Cryptogram Rhyme Q226

```
CODE = A B C D E F G H I J K L M N O P Q
       | | | | | | | | | | | | | | | | |
       I V P X H B Q K U A G Z C R J F S

       R S T U V W X Y Z
       | | | | | | | | |
       D L Y O W E M T N
```

The rhyme reads:

THE RAM, THE BULL, THE HEAVENLY TWINS
AND NEXT THE CRAB, THE LION SHINES,
THE VIRGIN AND THE SCALES,
THE SCORPION, ARCHER AND HE-GOAT,
THE MAN THAT BEARS THE WATERING-POT,
AND FISH WITH GLITTERING TAILS.

(Signs of the Zodiac.)

A224 Number Sequence 2 Q195
247 The 13th pentagonal number.

 1 = the 1st pentagonal number
 6 = the 2nd hexagonal number
18 = the 3rd heptagonal number
40 = the 4th octagonal number

The sequence then repeats itself to form a pattern with the 5th pentagonal number, the 6th hexagonal number, the 7th heptagonal number, the 8th octagonal number etc.

The following table shows the first seven of each of the above type of number.

Type of number	Formula	Number	1	2	3	4	5	6	7
Pentagonal	$\frac{1}{2}N(3N-1)$		1	5	12	22	35	51	70
Hexagonal	$\frac{1}{2}N(4N-2)$		1	6	15	28	45	66	91
Heptagonal	$\frac{1}{2}N(5N-3)$		1	7	18	34	55	81	112
Octagonal	$\frac{1}{2}N(6N-4)$		1	8	21	40	65	96	133

(N = Number, *e.g.* the 4th octagonal number = $\frac{1}{2}4(6 \times 4 - 4)$ = 40)

A225 Two in One Q166
1 Indestructable/understatement
2 Identification/responsibility
3 Advantageously/simplification
4 Apprenticeship/characteristic
5 Classification/diplomatically

A226 Prefix Q200
1 Eye; 2 Air; 3 Bed; 4 Soap; 5 Some; 6 Pass; 7 Ball;
8 Front; 9 Catch; 10 Moon; 11 Crack; 12 Corn

A227 Word Square Grid Q235

```
      H A M
      A G E
  T A M E N E T
  A P E   E R A
G A M E W   T A J A Y
A D O         A N I
M O D E E   W R Y I P
    E R F   R I A
    E F F L Y A K
      L E O
      Y O D
```

A228 Letter Grid – Heraldry Q217

Armed, Banderole, Barrulet, Blazoning, Boar, Cartouche, Chevronel, Couchant, Diapering, Embattled, Emblazon, Erminites, Erminois, Erne, Fret, Gorge, Hatchment, Herald, Kite, Lioncelle, Lozengy, Martlet, Naiant, Purpure, Regardant, Scutcheon, Sinople, Standard, Unicord.

This reveals 'Dieu Et Mon Droit'.

A229 'X' cluded Q183

M	B	F	O	E
P	Q	L	D	S
N	V	A	R	Z
W	C	I	G	H
Y	J	U	K	T

A230 Logic Path Q153
91

A231   Logic Box   Q171

C	G	B
F	A	E
H	D	I

A232   Group Puzzle   Q204
1 Fish, Whales, Poultry (a run of)
2 Cubs, Pigs, Whelps (a litter of)
3 Teal, Widgeon, Pochards (a knob or bunch of)
4 Cranes, Bitterns, Herons (a sedge/siege of)
5 Quails, Roes, Swans (a bevy of)
6 Seals, Goats, Curlews (a herd of)
Some words can be placed into more groups but the above solution
is the only way of arranging all into groups of three.

A233   Power Puzzle   Q220
A = 2; B = 4; C = 6; D = 7; E = 8; F = 0; G = 5

A234   Connection   Q191
$567^2 = 321489$
$854^2 = 729316$
Both equations use each of the digits 1 to 9 once each. These are
the only two numbers with this property.

A235   The Bottom Line   Q242
Reading from left to right:
289   308   267   284   301   262   279

A = 3   F = 7
B = 9   G = 5
C = 1   H = 6
D = 4   I = 8
E = 2   J = 0

All columns, rows and both diagonals total 1990.

A236 Letter Grid – Dogs Q209

Alsatian, Beagle, Bedlington, Blenheim, Cairn, Chihuahua, Cur, Dalmatian, Deerhound, Dhole, Great Dane, Greyhound, Husky, Lym, Pekinese, Pointer, Pomeranian, Pug, Rach, Ratter, Rug, Saluki, Schnauzer, Sheepdog, Spaniel.

The revealed word is Napoleon.

A237 Mix Up Thinkpower Q178

K	P	O	W	E	T	H	I	N	R
W	R	N	O	H	K	I	T	E	P
R	I	P	T	N	H	E	W	O	K
H	K	E	I	T	W	O	P	R	N
N	W	H	E	O	P	K	R	T	I
O	T	W	P	K	N	R	E	I	H
E	O	K	N	I	R	W	H	P	T
P	N	I	H	R	O	T	K	W	E
I	H	T	R	P	E	N	O	K	W
T	E	R	K	W	I	P	N	H	O

A238 Letter Sequence Q155

N.   The sequence is the first and last letter of the odd numbers starting with one.

The N completes eleven.

	A	B	C	D	E	F
A	1	3	2	1	6	5
B	5	4	2	1	2	3
C	6	4	2	3	3	4
D	1	1	5	6	5	4
E	3	6	2	3	1	4
F	2	5	6	4	5	6

A240 Letter Grid – Groups Q213

Bevy, brood, building, cast, charm, chattering, clowder, down, exaltation, flock, flush, gaggle, gathering, kindle, lepe, murder, murmuration, muster, nide, pack, paddling, school, skein, skulk, smuck, sounder, spring, swarm, wisp.

The revealed group name is shrewdness.

A241 Anagrams Q165

1 Anagrammatically; 2 Disqualification; 3 Misinterpretation;
4 Irresponsibility; 5 Prestidigitation; 6 Interchangeable;
7 Representational; 8 Misunderstanding; 9 Instrumentalist;
10 Antidisestablishmentarianism

A242 Number Sequence 1 Q194

5823 When the reverse of the number is subtracted from the original number, the same digits appear but in a different order. These are the only four-digit numbers to which this applies (the exception in the sequence is 1980).

A243 All Square Q234

```
G A R T E R
A V E R S E
R E C I T E
T R I B A L
E S T A T E
R E E L E R
```

A244 Group Puzzle Q203

The 15 four-letter words can be arranged to form five 12-letter words.

BACKSLAPPING DISCOVERABLE FEATHERBRAIN
FREETHINKING SELFSTARTING

A245 One Missing Q173

I	C	F
C	B	A
G	A	H

The small squares fit thus:

```
E G B
C F H
A I D
```

A246 What's in a Name? Q205

Frank, Ralph, Colin .....all types of bird.
Beryl, Hazel, Ruby ......all prefixes for colours. Beryl Blue,
Hazel Brown, Ruby Red.
Ellen, Glen, Douglas ....all English rivers.

A247 Letter Grid – Ports Q215

Adelaide, Cocanada, Cork, Damietta, Dunleary, Elat, Emden, Elsinore, Flushing, Galle, Genoa, Gisborne, Hakodate, Kakinada, Kiel, Kobe, Larvik, Macassar, Matarini, Moulmein, Mtwara, Nakhodka, Navarino, Osaka, Paradeep, Pula, Riga, Tamatave, Varna, Venice, Weihai, Yokohama.
The revealed port is Alexandria.

C	A	T	E	R	N	O	R	T	H
A	D	O	R	E	O	P	E	R	A
T	O	K	E	N	R	E	B	U	S
E	R	E	C	T	T	R	U	S	T
R	E	N	T	S	H	A	S	T	E
S	T	A	L	E	P	R	I	D	E
T	E	N	O	N	R	E	R	A	N
A	N	E	N	T	I	R	A	T	E
L	O	N	E	R	D	A	T	U	M
E	N	T	R	Y	E	N	E	M	Y

A249　Allsorts　Q199

The 16 words can be arranged into four groups of anagrams.
1 Alerting, integral, relating, triangle.
2 Catering, argentic, creating, reacting.
3 Estrange, greatens, reagents, sergeant.
4 Nitrates, intreats, straiten, tertians.

A250　Letter Sequence　Q159

E.　A is the first letter of the alphabet with symmetry about the vertical axis, B is the first letter of the alphabet with symmetry about the horizontal axis, H is the first letter of the alphabet with symmetry about the vertical and horizontal axis, and F is the first letter of the alphabet with no symmetry at all. The sequence then repeats with the second letter of the alphabet with symmetry about the vertical axis and so on.

A251   Mr Hoan   Q202
B and D.   Hoan is an anagram of Noah. If you place the word ark after each of the eight letters, a new 4-letter word is formed. H, L, S, P, N, M, B and D are the only letters to which this applies.

A252   The Square Cube   Q223
69   $69^2 = 4761$
     $69^3 = 328509$

A253   Anagram Blocks   Q168
A Disproportionately; B Comprehensibleness; C Establishmentarian; D Characteristically.